GREEN MOUNTAIN INTUITIVE ARTS

The Green Mountain Astrological Moon Journal 2021: an intuitive moon journal
Copyright © 2020-2021 by Mary Anna Abuzahra
Green Mountain Intuitive Arts
Plainfield, Vermont

Cover image: Mary Anna Abuzahra © 2020
Cover and Page design: Mary Anna Abuzahra, Green Mountain Intuitive Arts

Mary Anna is available for astrological sessions, astrological mentoring, presentations, lectures, and intuitive storytelling.

To contact author: info@greenmountainintuitivearts.com

The Green Mountain Astrological Moon Journal is a copyrighted document.
Mary Anna Abuzahra ©2020-21 Green Mountain Intuitive Arts

Library of Congress Control Number: 2020916904

ISBN, print: 978-0-578-75745-2

Printed in the United States of America through Lulu Press, a certified B Corporation

9780578757452

The Green Mountain Astrological Moon Journal
2021 UTC

Table of Contents

Overview

- This unique lunar-astrological journal includes fourteen lunar cycles, with astrological degrees of the sun and moon at each of the eight common phases.
    - The journal is calculated using the Tropical Zodiac and UTC (Coordinated Universal Time).
    - You can use the journal as a basic astrological moon journal without your natal chart.
    - For more personalization of the journal, you will need at least one copy of your accurate natal astrological chart that you can work with and/or make copies of. It is important that your chart be calculated with the accurate time of your birth to make best use of this journal process.
    - Personalize your journal entry for each moon phase, by identifying the astrological degree of each moon phase in your own natal astrological chart, choosing basic keywords for the natal house (noun) and the zodiac sign (adjective) to create a journal entry. This personalized journal sentence can be a starting point for further self-reflection.

- The moon cycle represents the cycle of growth of plant life, from germination to flower to seed.
    - This cycle of darkness and reflected light is imprinted within all life on Earth.
    - The repeating patterns light and darkness of the moon phases invites a personal reflection on our inner knowledge; helping to experience a state of intuitive listening and alignment with the ever-changing cycle of nature.

- Astrological knowledge is not necessary, although helpful!
    - If you are new to astrology you will be learning as you go, developing & deepening your knowledge of astrology through self-observation, journaling & engaging in your own life.
    - If you have more advanced astrological skills, bring your own resources and knowledge base to this focused work.
    - The sentences that you compose – your journal entries - can also be aligned with your favorite tarot or oracle deck, for further journaling, as stand- alone goals and/or meditations for each phase.

- Should you need a copy of your natal chart:
    - There are many free opportunities to get your chart and natal moon phase online.
    - Contact me through the website to order a digital file of natal chart small fee.
        - Date of birth, accurate time and location is needed. All personal data is kept in strict confidence. Specify your email address so that I can do my part to help keep your data confidential.

- Eclipses and Daily Ephemeris at Midnight UTC are included.
- Solstices and Equinoxes are posted on relevant ephemeris pages.

Disclaimer, Guidelines & Directions

Disclaimer:

A note about weaving intuition throughout your daily life: sometimes staying constantly in tune with intuition and empathic process can be overwhelming; a system of grounding and balance is required. Please find a grounding exercise that works for your individual needs. This journal process is not meant as a substitute for professional mental health or spiritual counseling.

Guidelines:

- How do events in your own life align with the signs and houses in your chart as the moon transits through them? Compose journal entries (sentences) to empower healthy choices in your life.
- Read Questions on Page 8 for each moon phase. These questions are common stages of change, and helpful to consider .They are also posted on each Journal Entry Page.
- For best accuracy in your daily life, convert each moon phase time & date for your time zone & Daylight Savings /Standard time in your own time zone. See page 135 for online links to several Time Conversion websites.
- The sun degrees are included as it is the light source for the reflected moonlight! At a new moon, the sun and moon are at the same degree. At other phases, the angle between the two bodies is essential to recognize. For example, an Aries Full Moon is typically a reflection a Libra Sun. A Libra Full Moon is typically a reflection of an Aries Sun. So, you can choose keywords from both Sun and Moon signs. It is helpful to track the yearly pattern of the sun in your chart as it is the same each year, yet the moon changes in a 19-year pattern.
- Eclipses are included in the Table of Contents as well as on corresponding Pages.
- Daily Ephemeris for the degrees of the Moon (at Midnight UTC) is posted for each moon cycle.
- Please contact the author should you need help getting up and running with your moon journal. I created this journal process in 1997 as a tool to align with the moon's cycle of growth, development and decline, and the powerful archetypes of the zodiac with expressive and intuitive journaling. I have worked as a professional astrologer for over 25 years, working with individual clients, presenting workshops, lectures, research, and creating tools for deeper learning. The author has offered this monthly journaling for groups and individuals since 1997. The Green Mountain Astrological Moon Journal is a copyrighted document.

Directions:

Step 1: Check Table of Contents for the page of the moon cycle that you need, such as Sagittarius 2020, or whichever cycle you are starting with. For best use, focus on the current cycle/phase that you are approaching at the time, or are current in at the time. There are 9 pages per moon cycle. Locate the New Moon Journal Entry page. Update the time (and date if necessary) from UTC to your local time. It will be the same +/- until Daylight Savings changes it by one hour forward, the same when your local standard time changes backward. Note the zodiac degree. Check your Natal Chart for this degree and write the Natal House number in the blank area next to "Natal House" across to the right on the line for "New".

Step 2: On the House Keywords column, choose at least one key word for the Natal House that you identified in Step 1. (Circle your keyword/s) This keyword functions as a noun in your sentence composition on new moon line on the Journal Entry Page. Choose words that resonate within you or relate to current trends in your life.

Example for a Natal Chart where the degree may be in the 12th House:

> **12th House: <u>concern for others,</u>** self-sacrifice, psychological
> health, escapism, drug use, pre-natal imprinting, secret keeping,
> surrender, spirituality

Step 3: On the New Moon Journal Entry page, note the Keywords for the zodiac sign and choose at least one keyword for the sign of the new moon. (Circle your keyword) This keyword will function as an adjective to the noun that you chose in your sentence building under new moon line. This sign and degree of the zodiac is the same for everyone, the House placement of the degree is your personal information. Choose words that resonate for you.

Step 4: On the Journal Entry Page, clarify your sentence for the New Moon Phase.
NOTE: Natal Phase Returns and Natal Degree Returns (check Ephemeris) are important to acknowledge, these are creative and fertile time frames during each moon cycle.

- "I emerge with (choose adjective/choose noun)." Example:

⬤ **New**   **January 13 5:00**   **Moon 23°♑13'**   **Natal House** _12th_
                                    Sun   **23°♑13'**

What am I open to for the upcoming cycle? What am I becoming aware of? What does my intuition bring? This is a contemplative outlook. Seedling/Germination
Moon & Sun in ♑ CAPRICORN: authoritative, disciplined, realistic, **<u>responsible,</u>** practical, goal oriented, materialistic, **<u>successful</u>**, ambitious, professional, manifesting

"I emerge with _responsible & successful approach to my psychological health._

STEP 5: Continue to journal your intuitive thoughts/experiences and choose a tarot card or other oracle or inspirational card or object and journal using your intuition of how this ties into your journal entry at the top of the page. Repeat these steps for each moon phase. For all phases except NEW, include the Sun's placement in your journaling process. Please note that the VERB for each phase is different, in alignment with the growth and decay of light of the entire cycle.
Example: Crescent Phase is: **"I challenge myself to…."**

Please add in your own cultural, religious, and/or seasonal celebrations to your journaling.

Eclipses: dates and times are included and align with New and Full Moons. Eclipses can help with changes to bring in or move out things in our lives whether the eclipse is visible where we live or not. Please see table of contents for eclipse dates.

Importance of Your Natal Moon Phase & Natal Degree

- Your natal moon phase is an important key to understanding your natal chart. Knowledge of your natal moon phase can suggest a life-long approach or attitude that is helpful for you as well as others around you.

- Your natal moon phase is derived from the angle between the Sun and Moon at the time of your birth. Use this online Moon Phase Calculator if you do not know your natal moon phase. Moon Phase Calculator: https://www.timeanddate.com/moon/phases/

- During each moon cycle, you can use our own natal recurring phase as a strong point during the cycle and schedule important activities or self-care during those few days. If you know the exact angle, you can pinpoint it each Month to the exact day and time, which is a creative time frame and has been linked to conception/fertility.

- Your Natal Moon Zodiac Degree is also a key to understanding more about your chart and moon cycles. This degree repeats each moon phase and knowing the day each Month has also been linked to conception and fertility.

- If you are interested in learning more about what your natal moon phase means, you can order a related consultation with the author.

Moon Phase Reference

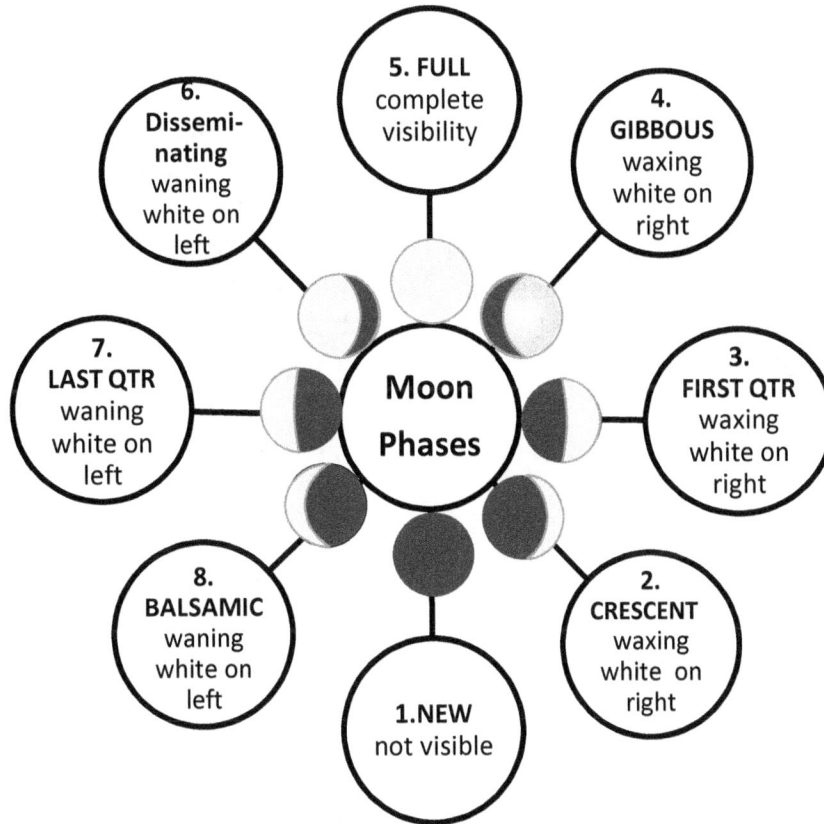

New: Emergence, Germination, 0-45° angle to Sun Winter Solstice/Moon & Sun conjoin/☽ ☌ ☉

Crescent: Struggle, Seedling, 45-90° angle to Sun: Semi-squares Sun, separating/☽ ∠ ☉ s

1st QTR: Action, Leaf/Stem/Root, 90-135° angle Sun Squares Sun, separating/☽ □ ☉ s

Gibbous: Structure, Bud, 135-180° angle to Sun Sesquisquare Sun, separating/☽ ⚼ ☉ S

Full: Fulfillment, Flower/Fruit, 180-225° angle to Sun Opposes Sun/☽ ☍ ☉

Disseminating: Share, Harvest, 225-270° angle to Sun Sesquisquare Sun approaching/ ☽ ⚼ ☉

Last QTR: Reorient, Decay, 270-315° angle to Sun: Square Sun, approaching/ ☽ □ ☉

Balsamic: Release/Resolve, Seed, 315-360° angle to Sun Semi-square Sun, approaching/☽ ∠ ☉

Astrological Reference

Signs & Correlations, abbreviations

♈ **ARIES**-assertive-1st House -Ar
♉ **TAURUS**-ownership-2nd House -Ta
♊ **GEMINI**-communication-3rd House-Ge
♋ **CANCER**-home-family-4th House-Cn
♌ **LEO**-selfexpression-5th House-Le
♍ **VIRGO**-routines-6th House-Vi

♎ **LIBRA**-partnerships-7th House-Li
♏ **SCORPIO**-deep sharing-8th House-Sc
♐ **SAGITTARIUS**-truthseeking-9thHouse-Sg
♑ **CAPRICORN**-authority-10th House-Cp
♒ **AQUARIUS**-friends & groups-11th House-Aq
♓ **PISCES**-immersion, prenatal-12th House-Pi

Planets:

☉ **SUN**-identity
☽ **MOON**-emotion
☿ **MERCURY**-communication
♀ **VENUS**-values
♂ **MARS**-action

♃ **JUPITER**-expansion
♄ **SATURN**-restriction
♅ **URANUS**-uniqueness
♆ **NEPTUNE**-creativity

Asteroids and Dwarf Planets

⚷ **CHIRON**-weakness into strength
⚴ **PALLAS ATHENA**-strategy
♇ **PLUTO**-transformation

⚶ **VESTA**-sacred focus
⚵ **JUNO**-partnering
⚳ **CERES** – nourishment

Modalities

CARDINAL: Aries/Cancer/Libra/Capricorn   **FIXED:** Taurus/Leo/Scorpio/Aquarius
MUTABLE: Gemini/Virgo/Sagittarius/Pisces

More:

⊗   **PART OF FORTUNE** –physical connection to surroundings/environment
ASC   **ASCENDENT:** presentation of self/mask (1st Hse Cusp)("Rising Sign")
MC   **MIDHEAVEN:** worldly impression of self/career (10th Hse Cusp)
DES   **DESCENDENT:** partner/projection onto partner (7th Hse Cusp)
IC   **INUM CEOLI:** family roots/ancestry (4th Hse Cusp)
NODES OF THE MOON: ☊ **North**-destiny   ☋ **South**-past life skills

Keywords Houses and Signs

Adjectives	Nouns
♈ **ARIES:** assertive, courageous, independent, passionate, athletic, enthusiastic, active, aggressive, initiating, direct, angry, bullying	**1st House:** my body, my identity, myself, my appearance, my projected image, my soul-purpose, initial approach to life, my interests, my sense of me
♉ **TAURUS:** sensual, reliable, valuable, consistent, resourceful, deliberate, passive, practical, financial, comfortable, stubborn	**2nd House:** my talents, my resources, my values, my physical possessions, my money, my personal self-esteem, my sensuous enjoyment, my self-worth
♊ **GEMINI:** Clever, versatile, alert, cheerful, curious, articulate, adaptable, lighthearted, happy, quick-witted, cheerful, talkative	**3rd House:** my adaptability, my communications, my siblings, my neighborhood, short journey, my active search for knowledge, learning, curiosity, thinking
♋ **CANCER:** nurturing, attached, emotional, protective, psychic, domestic, intuitive, psychic, sensitive, supportive, possessive	**4th House:** my home, family, heritage, my privacy, my emotional life, feelings, eating habits, receptivity, my protective urges, vulnerability
♌ **LEO:** self-confident, dignified, generous, playful, dramatic, courageous, caring, romantic, loving, brave, self-centered, egotistical	**5th House:** my creative abilities, my self-expression pregnancy, children, pleasures, will power, romance, merry making, vacation, affection, confidence
♍ **VIRGO:** analytical, organized, efficient, health-conscious, conscientious, exacting, technical, healing, discriminating, picky	**6th House:** my work conditions & habits, pets, my health, service offered, productivity, training, work skills, hygiene, clothing, nutrition & diet
♎ **LIBRA:** cooperative, fair, considerate, artistic, tasteful, diplomatic, tactful, impartial, refined, balanced, deliberate, soft-spoken, judgmental	**7th House:** agreements, contracts, partnerships, spouse, relationships, consultants, open enemies, receiving love, self-projection, social skills
♏ **SCORPIO:** transformational, mysterious, hidden, sexual, erotic, secretive, musical, trust-worthy, loyal, supportive, jealous	**8th House:** loyalty, partner's money & resources, taxes, inheritance, psychic & occult, transformation, shared values, sexual energy, investigations
♐ **SAGITTARIUS:** expansive, philosophical, truth seeking, ethical, idealistic, optimistic, inspiring, wise, motivational, truth speaking, honest	**9th House:** wisdom, justice, law, exploration, faith, religious & spiritual, higher education, foreign travel, legal action, experimentation, truth seeking
♑ **CAPRICORN:** authoritative, disciplined, realistic, responsible, practical, goal oriented, materialistic, successful, ambitious, professional,	**10th House:** accomplishments, authority, recognition, success, reputation, professional affairs, maturity, mastery, honor, self-fulfillment, public image/life
♒ **AQUARIUS:** humanitarian, collective, innovative, progressive, eccentric, detached, electric, friendly, generous, gregarious, aloof	**11th House:** groups & clubs, trends, friends, political awareness, emotional detachment, progressive thought, new technology & inventions, astrology
♓ **PISCES:** spiritual, subtle, empathic, visionary, sensitive, psychic, vulnerable, intuitive, self-sacrificing, indulgent, loving, artistic	**12th House:** concern for others, self-sacrifice, psychological health, escapism, drug use, pre-natal imprinting, secret keeping, surrender, spirituality

Questions, Outlook, Life Cycle & Stages of Change

Listed below are open ended questions, outlook
And the corresponding stages of change and plant life cycle.

New Moon: Emerge – ask: What am I open to for the upcoming cycle? What am I becoming aware of? This is a contemplative stage. Germination is complete, sprouting begins

Crescent Moon: Promise/struggle/Challenge-ask: What are the things I want to overcome? What resources do I need? How do I prepare? What am I resisting? This is a preparation stage. Sprout becomes a seedling

First Qtr: Action- ask: What are the steps I need to take to accomplish my goals? How do I move forward? This is a stage of action. Roots, stem, and leaves appear & photosynthesis is strong

Waxing Gibbous: Perfect and structure- ask: How do I stay on track? What do I need to stay organized? What do I need to compromise if anything? This is a maintenance stage. Buds appear and develop in size.

Full: Reflect and fulfill –ask: How do I see myself functioning in my world with my process? What does it look like within me and in my day to day world? This is a reflective stage. Flower blooms appear.

Disseminating/Waning Gibbous: Share – ask: How can I best share my experiences? Where can I help others with my learning and experience? This is a stage of sharing. First harvest, fruit is shared

Last Qtr: Reorient – ask: How do I change or let go of the patterns that do not serve me and/or my community? This is a reorienting stage. Last harvest and turning under of plant for composting.

Balsamic: Release, resolve, plan – ask: How do I resolve the past Month and visualize, plan for up upcoming process? This is a contemplative stage. Seed is planted, released to develop next cycle/ germination begins.

♏ Scorpio 2020 Lunar Eclipse

EPHEMERIS at Midnight UTC		Chart House keywords are nouns.
		1st House: my body, my identity, myself, my appearance, my projected image, my soul-purpose, my initial approach to life, my interests, my sense of me
15-Nov	20°Sc03'	
16-Nov	05°Sg08'	
17-Nov	19°Sg58'	**2nd House:** my talents, my resources, my values, my physical possessions, my Mooney, my personal self-esteem, my sensuous enjoyment, my self-worth
18-Nov	04°Cp25'	
19-Nov	18°Cp26'	**3rd House:** my adaptability, my communications, my siblings, my neighborhood, short journey, my active search for knowledge, learning, curiosity, thinking
20-Nov	01°Aq59'	
21-Nov	15°Aq07'	
22-Nov	27°Aq51'	**4th House:** my home, family, heritage, my privacy, my emotional life, feelings, eating habits, receptivity, my protective urges, vulnerability
23-Nov	10°Pi16'	
24-Nov	22°Pi26'	**5th House:** my abilities, my creative ability, pregnancy, children, pleasures, will power, romance, merry making, vacation, affection, confidence
25-Nov	04°Ar26'	
26-Nov	16°Ar19'	
27-Nov	28°Ar10'	**6th House:** my work conditions & habits, pets, my health, service offered, productivity, training, work skills, hygiene, clothing, nutrition & diet
28-Nov	10°Ta00'	
29-Nov	21°Ta53'	**7th House:** agreements, contracts, partnerships, spouse, relationships, consultants, open enemies, receiving love, self-projection, social skills
30-Nov	03°Ge52'	
1-Dec	15°Ge57'	
2-Dec	28°Ge10'	**8th House:** loyalty, partner's Mooney & resources, taxes, inheritance, psychic & occult matters, transformation, shared values, sexual energy, investigations
3-Dec	10°Cn34'	
4-Dec	23°Cn09'	
5-Dec	05°Le58'	**9th House:** wisdom, justice, law, exploration, faith, religious & spiritual pursuits, higher education, foreign travel, legal action, experimentation, seeking truth
6-Dec	19°Le01'	
7-Dec	02°Vi22'	**10th House:** accomplishments, authority, recognition, success, reputation, professional affairs, maturity, mastery, honor, self-fulfillment, public life
8-Dec	16°Vi01'	
9-Dec	29°Vi59'	
10-Dec	14°Li15'	**11th House:** groups & clubs, trends, friends, political awareness, emotional detachment, progressive thought, new technology & inventions, astrology
11-Dec	28°Li47'	
12-Dec	13°Sc31'	**12th House:** concern for others, self-sacrifice, psychological health, pre-natal imprinting, secret keeping, surrender, acceptance, spirituality
13-Dec	28°Sc21'	
14-Dec	13°Sg10'	

New   **November 15, 2020**   05:07 **Moon 23°♏ 17'**   **Natal House_____**
                                                                 Sun   23°♏ 17'

What am I open to for the upcoming cycle? What is entering my awareness? What does my intuition bring? This is a contemplative outlook. Seedling/Germination

Moon & Sun in ♏ SCORPIO: transformational, magnetic, mysterious, hidden, sexual, erotic, secretive, musical, renewing, trust-worthy, loyal, supportive

I emerge with

_____

_____

_____

_____

_____

_____

_____

_____

My Tarot, Oracle, or Inspiration Card for New Moon Phase: _____

_____

_____

_____

_____

_____

_____

_____

_____

Crescent   **November 18, 2020**   **12:12** **Moon 11°♑36'**   **Natal House_____**
                                                            Sun   26°♏36'   **Natal House_____**

What will I overcome that is worth letting go of? What are my resources? How do I prepare? What change am I resisting? This is preparedness outlook. Sprout

Moon in ♑ CAPRICORN: authoritative, disciplined, realistic, responsible, practical, goal oriented, materialistic, successful, ambitious, professional, manifesting

Sun in ♏ SCORPIO: transformational, magnetic, mysterious, hidden, sexual, erotic, secretive, musical, renewing, trust-worthy, loyal, supportive

I challenge myself to

_____

_____

_____

_____

_____

_____

_____

_____

_____

_____

My Tarot, Oracle, or Inspiration Card for Crescent Phase: _____

_____

_____

_____

_____

_____

_____

_____

First Quarter   November 22, 2020 04:44 Moon 00°♓20'   Natal House_____
                                          Sun   00°♐20'   Natal House_____

What steps will I take toward accomplishing my goals? How do I move forward in the next few days and/or long term? This is an action outlook. Root/Stem/Leaf – photosynthesis strengthens.
Moon in ♓ PISCES: ♓ **PISCES:** spiritual, subtle, empathic, visionary, sensitive, psychic, vulnerable, intuitive, self-sacrificing, indulgent, loving, artistic
Sun in ♐ SAGITTARIUS: expansive, philosophical, truth seeking, ethical, idealistic, optimistic, inspiring, wise, truth-seeking, motivational, truth speaking, honest

I take action on

_____
_____
_____
_____
_____
_____
_____
_____

My Tarot, Oracle, or Inspirational Card for First Quarter Phase: _____

_____
_____
_____
_____
_____
_____
_____

How do I stay on track? What do I need to stay organized? What do I need to compromise if anything? This is a maintenance outlook. Buds appear and develop in size.

Moon in ♈ ARIES: assertive, courageous, independent, passionate, athletic, enthusiastic, active, aggressive, initiating, focused, forward, direct

Sun in ♐ SAGITTARIUS: expansive, philosophical, truth seeking, ethical, idealistic, optimistic, inspiring, wise, truth-seeking, motivational, truth speaking, honest

I develop structure with

_____

_____

_____

_____

_____

_____

_____

_____

My Tarot, Oracle, or Inspirational Card for Gibbous Phase: _____

_____

_____

_____

_____

_____

_____

_____

_____

LUNAR ECLIPSE

Full   November 30 2020 09:29   Moon 08° Ⅱ 38'   Natal House_____

Sun   08° ⚹ 38'   Natal House_____

How do I see myself functioning in my world with my process? What does it look like within me and in my day to day world? This is a reflective outlook. Flower/Fruit

Moon in Ⅱ GEMINI: Clever, versatile, agile, curious, articulate, alert, conversational, adaptable, lighthearted, happy, quick-witted, cheerful

Sun in ⚹ SAGITTARIUS: expansive, philosophical, truth seeking, ethical, idealistic, optimistic, inspiring, wise, truth-seeking, motivational, truth speaking, honest

I reflect fulfillment with

_____

_____

_____

_____

_____

_____

_____

_____

My Tarot, Oracle, or Inspirational Card for Full Moon Phase: _____

_____

_____

_____

_____

_____

_____

◐ **Disseminating**　　**December 4 2020　08:27　Moon 27°♋38'**　　　　**Natal House** _____

　　　　　　　　　　　　　　　　　　　Sun　　12°♐38'　　　　**Natal House** _____

How can I share my experiences? Where can I help others with my learning and experience?
This is a sharing outlook. First harvest.

Moon in ♋ CANCER: nurturing, family oriented, watery, emotional, protective, psychic, domestic, sustaining, intuitive, sensitive, nurturing

Sun in ♐ SAGITTARIUS: expansive, philosophical, truth seeking, ethical, idealistic, optimistic, inspiring, wise, truth-seeking, motivational, truth speaking, honest

I share

_____

_____

_____

_____

_____

_____

_____

My Tarot, Oracle, or Inspirational Card for Disseminating Phase: _____

_____

_____

_____

_____

_____

_____

◑ **Last Quarter**　　　**December 8 2020　00:36**　　**Moon 16°♍22'**　　__Natal House_____
　　　　　　　　　　　　　　　　　　　　　　　Sun　16°♐22'　　**Natal House_____**

How do I change or let go of the patterns that do not serve me and/or my community?
This is a reorienting outlook. Decay/Last Harvest and turning under of plant remains for composting.
Moon in ♍ VIRGO: analytical, organized, efficient, health-conscious, conscientious, exacting, technical, healing, problem solving, scientific, time efficient
Sun in ♐ SAGITTARIUS: expansive, philosophical, truth seeking, ethical, idealistic, optimistic, inspiring, wise, truth-seeking, motivational, truth speaking, honest

I change perspective on

_____

_____

_____

_____

_____

_____

_____

My Tarot, Oracle, or Inspirational Card for Last Quarter Phase:_____

_____

_____

_____

_____

_____

_____

Balsamic   December 11 2020   09:49   Moon 04°♏48'   Natal House _____

                                                          Sun   19°♐48'   Natal House _____

How do I resolve the past Month and visualize, plan for up upcoming process? This is a pre-contemplative outlook. Seed is planted, released to develop next cycle/ germination begins.

Moon in ♏ SCORPIO: transformational, magnetic, mysterious, hidden, sexual, erotic, secretive, musical, renewing, trust-worthy, loyal, supportive

Sun in ♐ SAGITTARIUS: expansive, philosophical, truth seeking, ethical, idealistic, optimistic, inspiring, wise, truth-seeking, motivational, truth speaking, honest

I resolve/release and/or plan

_____

_____

_____

_____

_____

_____

_____

_____

My Tarot, Oracle, or Inspirational Card for the Balsamic Phase: _____

_____

_____

_____

_____

_____

_____

_____

♐ Sagittarius 2020 Total Solar Eclipse

EPHEMERIS at Midnight UTC		Chart House keywords are nouns.
14-Dec	13°Sg10'	
15-Dec	27°Sg50'	**1st House:** my body, my identity, myself, my appearance, my projected image, my soul-purpose, my initial approach to life, my interests, my sense of me
16-Dec	12°Cp14'	
17-Dec	26°Cp17'	
18-Dec	09°Aq56'	**2nd House:** my talents, my resources, my values, my physical possessions, my money, my personal self-esteem, my sensuous enjoyment, my self-worth
19-Dec	23°Aq11'	
20-Dec	06°Pi01'	
Solstice 21-Dec	18°Pi31'	**3rd House:** my adaptability, my communications, my siblings, my neighborhood, short journey, my active search for knowledge, learning, curiosity, thinking
22-Dec	00°Ar44'	
23-Dec	12°Ar44'	**4th House:** my home, family, heritage, my privacy, my emotional life, feelings, eating habits, receptivity, my protective urges, vulnerability
24-Dec	24°Ar37'	
25-Dec	06°Ta26'	
26-Dec	18°Ta17'	**5th House:** my abilities, my creative ability, pregnancy, children, pleasures, will power, romance, merry making, vacation, affection, confidence
27-Dec	00°Ge13'	
28-Dec	12°Ge18'	
29-Dec	24°Ge34'	**6th House:** my work conditions & habits, pets, my health, service offered, productivity, training, work skills, hygiene, clothing, nutrition & diet
30-Dec	07°Cn03'	
31-Dec	19°Cn47'	
Jan 1 2021	02°Le44'	**7th House:** agreements, contracts, partnerships, spouse, relationships, consultants, open enemies, receiving love, self-projection, social skills
Jan 2 2021	15°Le55'	
Jan 3 2021	29°Le19'	
Jan 4 2021	12°Vi55'	**8th House:** loyalty, partner's money & resources, taxes, inheritance, psychic & occult matters, transformation, shared values, sexual energy, investigations
Jan 5 2021	26°Vi42'	
Jan 6 2021	10°Li39'	**9th House:** wisdom, justice, law, exploration, faith, religious & spiritual pursuits, higher education, foreign travel, legal action, experimentation, seeking truth
Jan 7 2021	24°Li44'	
Jan 8 2021	08°Sc57'	
Jan 9 2021	23°Sc16'	**10th House:** accomplishments, authority, recognition, success, reputation, professional affairs, maturity, mastery, honor, self-fulfillment, public life
Jan 10 2021	07°Sg37'	
Jan 11 2021	21°Sg58'	
Jan 12 2021	06°Cp13'	**11th House:** groups & clubs, trends, friends, political awareness, emotional detachment, progressive thought, new technology & inventions, astrology
Jan 13 2021	20°Cp18'	
		12th House: concern for others, self-sacrifice, psychological health, pre-natal imprinting, secret keeping, surrender, acceptance, spirituality

SOLAR ECLIPSE
New   **December 14 2020   16:16   Moon 23°♐08'**   **Natal House_____**
                                                          Sun   23°♐08'

What am I open to for the upcoming cycle? What is entering my awareness? What does my intuition bring? This is a contemplative outlook. Seedling/Germination

Moon & Sun in ♐ SAGITTARIUS: expansive, philosophical, truth seeking, ethical, idealistic, optimistic, inspiring, wise, truth-seeking, motivational

I emerge with

_____

_____

_____

_____

_____

_____

_____

My Tarot, Oracle, or Inspiration Card for New Moon Phase: _____

_____

_____

_____

_____

_____

_____

_____

19

Crescent   December 18 2020 03:02 Moon 11°♒38'   Natal House_____
                                         Sun   26°♐38'   Natal House_____

What will I overcome that is worth letting go of? What are my resources? How do I prepare?What change am I resisting? This is preparedness outlook. Sprout

Moon in ♒ AQUARIUS: humanitarian, collective, innovative, progressive, eccentric, detached, electric, friendly, generous, gregarious, unpredictable, aloof

Sun in ♐ SAGITTARIUS: expansive, philosophical, truth seeking, ethical, idealistic, optimistic, inspiring, wise, truth-seeking, motivational

I challenge myself to

_____

_____

_____

_____

_____

_____

_____

_____

_____

My Tarot, Oracle, or Inspiration Card for Crescent Phase: _____

_____

_____

_____

_____

_____

_____

_____

First Quarter   December 21 2020   23:41   Moon 00°♈34'   Natal House_____
                                                    Sun   00°♑34'   Natal House_____

What steps will I take toward accomplishing my goals? How do I move forward in the next few days and/or long term? This is an action outlook. Root/Stem/Leaf – photosynthesis strengthens.
Moon in ♈ARIES: assertive, courageous, independent, passionate, athletic, enthusiastic, active, aggressive, initiating, focused, forward, direct
Sun in ♑ CAPRICORN: authoritative, disciplined, realistic, responsible, practical, goal oriented, materialistic, successful, ambitious, professional, manifesting

I take action on
_____

_____

_____

_____

_____

_____

_____

My Tarot, Oracle, or Inspirational Card for First Quarter Phase: _____

_____

_____

_____

_____

_____

_____

_____

Gibbous   December 26 2020   03:02   Moon 19°♉47′   Natal House_____

                                                  Sun   04°♑47′   Natal House_____

How do I stay on track? What do I need to stay organized? What do I need to compromise if anything?
This is a maintenance outlook. Buds appear and develop in size.

Moon in ♉ TAURUS: sensual, physical, reliable, consistent, resourceful, deliberate, passive, practical, sensual, financial, valued, comfortable

Sun in ♑ CAPRICORN: authoritative, disciplined, realistic, responsible, practical, goal oriented, materialistic, successful, ambitious, professional, manifesting

I develop structure with

_____

_____

_____

_____

_____

_____

_____

My Tarot, Oracle, or Inspirational Card for Gibbous Phase: _____

_____

_____

_____

_____

_____

_____

_____

Full   **December 30 2020**   03:28   **Moon** 08°♋53'   **Natal House**_____

                                                     Sun 08°♑53'   **Natal House**_____

How do I see myself functioning in my world with my process? What does it look like within me and in my day to day world? This is a reflective outlook. Flower/Fruit

Moon in ♋ CANCER: nurturing, family oriented, watery, emotional, protective, psychic, domestic, sustaining, intuitive, sensitive, supportive, attached/connected

Sun in ♑ CAPRICORN: authoritative, disciplined, realistic, responsible, practical, goal oriented, materialistic, successful, ambitious, professional, manifesting ‗

I reflect fulfillment with

_____

_____

_____

_____

_____

_____

My Tarot, Oracle, or Inspirational Card for Full Moon Phase: _____

_____

_____

_____

_____

_____

_____

_____

_____

2021 BEGINS

◗ Disseminating   January 2 2021 21:06   Moon 27°♌41'   Natal House _____

                                                        Sun   12°♑41'   Natal House _____

How can I share my experiences? Where can I help others with my learning and experience? this is a sharing outlook. First harvest.

Moon in ♌ **LEO:** self-confident, dignified, generous, playful, dramatic, courageous, caring, radiant, romantic, loving, generous, self-centered, strong

Sun in ♑ **CAPRICORN:** authoritative, disciplined, realistic, responsible, practical, goal oriented, materialistic, successful, ambitious, professional, manifesting

I share _____

_____

_____

_____

_____

_____

_____

_____

my Tarot, Oracle, or Inspirational Card for Disseminating Phase: _____

_____

_____

_____

_____

_____

_____

_____

_____

Last Quarter   **January 6 2021**   **09:37**   **Moon 16°♎17'**   **Natal House** _____
                                                    Sun   16°♑17'   **Natal House** _____

How do I change or let go of the patterns that do not serve me and/or my community?
This is a reorienting outlook. Decay/Last Harvest and turning under of plant remains for composting.
Moon in ♎ LIBRA: cooperative, fair, considerate, artistic, tasteful, diplomatic, tactful, impartial, refined, balanced, deliberate, soft-spoken, judgmental
Sun in ♑ CAPRICORN: authoritative, disciplined, realistic, responsible, practical, goal oriented, materialistic, successful, ambitious, professional, manifesting

I change perspective on
_____

_____

_____

_____

_____

_____

_____

_____

My Tarot, Oracle, or Inspirational Card for Last Quarter Phase:_____

_____

_____

_____

_____

_____

_____

_____

Balsamic   **January 9 2021 19:11**   **Moon 04° ♐ 44'**   **Natal House** _____

                                                   Sun   19° ♑ 44'   **Natal House** _____

How do I resolve the past Month and visualize, plan for up upcoming process? This is a pre-contemplative outlook. Seed is planted, released to develop next cycle/ germination begins.

Moon in ♐ SAGITTARIUS: expansive, philosophical, truth seeking, ethical, idealistic, optimistic, inspiring, wise, truth-seeking, motivational, truth speaking, honest

Sun in ♑ CAPRICORN: authoritative, disciplined, realistic, responsible, practical, goal oriented, materialistic, successful, ambitious, professional, manifesting

I resolve/release and/or plan

_____

_____

_____

_____

_____

_____

_____

_____

My Tarot, Oracle, or Inspirational Card for the Balsamic Phase: _____

_____

_____

_____

_____

_____

_____

_____

_____

♑ Capricorn 2021

Ephemeris at Midnight UTC		Keywords for Natal Chart Houses (House keywords are nouns)
		1st House: my body, my identity, myself, my appearance, my projected image, my soul-purpose, my initial approach to life, my interests, my sense of me
13-Jan	20°Cp18'	
14-Jan	04°Aq09'	
15-Jan	17°Aq43'	**2nd House:** my talents, my resources, my values, my physical possessions, my money, my personal self-esteem, my sensuous enjoyment, myself worth
16-Jan	00°Pi55'	
17-Jan	13°Pi48'	
18-Jan	26°Pi20'	**3rd House:** my adaptability, my communications, my siblings, my neighborhood, short journey, my active search for knowledge, learning, curiosity, thinking
19-Jan	08°Ar35'	
20-Jan	20°Ar37'	
21-Jan	02°Ta30'	**4th House:** my home, family, , heritage, my privacy, my emotional life, feelings, eating habits, receptivity, my protective urges, vulnerability
22-Jan	14°Ta19'	
23-Jan	26°Ta10'	**5th House:** my abilities, my creative ability, pregnancy, children, pleasures, will power, romance, merry making, vacation, affection, confidence,
24-Jan	08°Ge07'	
25-Jan	20°Ge16'	
26-Jan	02°Cn40'	**6th House:** my work conditions & habits, pets, my health, service offered, productivity, training, work skills, hygiene, clothing, nutrition & diet
27-Jan	15°Cn22'	
28-Jan	28°Cn24'	
29-Jan	11°Le44'	**7th House:** agreements, contracts, partnerships, spouse, relationships, consultants, open enemies, receiving love, self-projection, social skills
30-Jan	25°Le22'	
31-Jan	09°Vi14'	
1-Feb	23°Vi16'	**8th House:** loyalty, partner's money & resources, taxes, inheritance, psychic & occult matters, transformation, shared values, sexual energy, investigations
2-Feb	07°Li25'	
3-Feb	21°Li35'	**9th House:** wisdom, justice, law, exploration, faith, religious & spiritual pursuits, higher education, foreign travel, legal action, experimentation, seeking truth
4-Feb	05°Sc45'	
5-Feb	19°Sc52'	
6-Feb	03°Sg55'	**10th House:** accomplishments, authority, recognition, success, reputation, professional affairs, maturity, mastery, honor, self-fulfillment, public life
7-Feb	17°Sg54'	
8-Feb	01°Cp48'	
9-Feb	15°Cp35'	**11th House:** groups & clubs, trends, friends, political awareness, emotional detachment, progressive thought, new technology & inventions, astrology
10-Feb	29°Cp14'	
11-Feb	12°Aq42'	
		12th House: concern for others, self-sacrifice, psychological health, pre-natal imprinting, secret keeping, surrender, acceptance, spirituality

New   January 13 2021   05:00   Moon 23°♑13'   Natal House _____
                                                                    Sun   23°♑13'

What am I open to for the upcoming cycle? What is entering my awareness? What does my intuition bring? This is a contemplative outlook. Seedling/Germination

Moon & Sun in ♑ CAPRICORN: authoritative, disciplined, realistic, responsible, practical, goal oriented, materialistic, successful, ambitious, professional, manifesting

I emerge with

_____

_____

_____

_____

_____

My Tarot, Oracle, or Inspirational Card for New Moon Phase: _____

_____

_____

_____

_____

_____

_____

_____

Crescent　　**January 16 2021**　　20:29　**Moon 11°♓56'**　　**Natal House**_____

Sun　26°♑56'　　**Natal House**_____

What will I overcome that is worth letting go of? What are my resources? How do I prepare? What change am I resisting? This is preparedness outlook. Sprout

Moon in ♓ PISCES: spiritual, subtle, empathic, visionary, sensitive, psychic, vulnerable, intuitive, self-sacrificing, indulgent, loving, artistic

Sun in ♑ CAPRICORN: authoritative, disciplined, realistic, responsible, practical, goal oriented, materialistic, successful, ambitious, professional, manifesting

I challenge myself to

_____

_____

_____

_____

_____

_____

_____

_____

_____

My Tarot, Oracle, or Inspiration Card for Crescent Phase: _____

_____

_____

_____

_____

_____

_____

First Quarter   **January 20 2021   21:01   Moon   01°♉01'   Natal House_____**
                                                    Sun   01°♒01'   Natal House_____

What steps will I take toward accomplishing my goals? How do I move forward in the next few days and/or long term? This is an action outlook. Root/Stem/Leaf – photosynthesis strengthens.

Moon in ♉ TAURUS: sensual, physical, reliable, consistent, resourceful, deliberate, passive, practical, sensual, financial, valued, comfortable

Sun in ♒ AQUARIUS: humanitarian, collective, innovative, progressive, eccentric, detached, electric, friendly, generous, gregarious, unpredictable, aloof

I take action on _____

_____

_____

_____

_____

_____

_____

My Tarot, Oracle, or Inspirational Card for First Quarter Phase: _____

_____

_____

_____

_____

_____

Gibbous   **January 24 2021**   **23:53 Moon 20°♊13'**   **Natal House_____**

Sun   05°♒13'   Natal House_____

How do I stay on track? What do I need to stay organized? What do I need to compromise if anything?
This is a maintenance outlook. Buds appear and develop in size.

Moon in ♊ GEMINI: Clever, versatile, agile, curious, articulate, alert, conversational, adaptable, lighthearted, happy, quick-witted, cheerful

Sun in ♒ AQUARIUS: humanitarian, collective, innovative, progressive, eccentric, detached, electric, friendly, generous, gregarious, unpredictable, aloof

I develop structure with

_____

_____

_____

_____

_____

_____

_____

My Tarot, Oracle, or Inspirational Card for Gibbous Phase: _____

_____

_____

_____

_____

_____

◯ **Full**   **January 28 2021**   **19:16 Moon 09°♌05'**   **Natal House**_____
                                              Sun   09°♒05'   **Natal House**_____

How do I see myself functioning in my world with my process? What does it look like within me and in my day to day world? This is a reflective outlook. Flower/Fruit

Moon in ♌ LEO: self-confident, dignified, generous, playful, dramatic, courageous, caring, radiant, romantic, loving, self-centered/focused, strong hearted, brave

Sun in ♒AQUARIUS: humanitarian, collective, innovative, progressive, eccentric, detached, electric, friendly, generous, gregarious, unpredictable, aloof

I reflect fulfillment with

_____

_____

_____

_____

_____

_____

_____

My Tarot, Oracle, or Inspirational Card for Full Moon Phase:_____

_____

_____

_____

_____

_____

_____

◗ **Disseminating**   **February 1 2021**   07:25   **Moon 27°♍39'**   **Natal House** _____
                                                  Sun   12°♒39'   **Natal House** _____

How can I share my experiences? Where can I help others with my learning and experience?
This is a sharing outlook. First harvest.
Moon in ♍ VIRGO: analytical, organized, efficient, health-conscious, conscientious, exacting,
technical, healing, problem solving, scientific, time efficient
Sun in ♒ AQUARIUS: humanitarian, collective, innovative, progressive, eccentric, detached,
electric, friendly, generous, gregarious, unpredictable, aloof

I share _____

_____

_____

_____

_____

_____

_____

_____

My Tarot, Oracle, or Inspirational Card for Disseminating Phase: _____

_____

_____

_____

_____

_____

_____

_____

Last Quarter   **February 4 2021 17:36**   **Moon 16°♏ 07'**   **Natal House** _____
                                                                                                  Sun   16°♒ 07'   **Natal House** _____

How do I change or let go of the patterns that do not serve me and/or my community?
This is a reorienting outlook. Decay/Last Harvest and turning under of plant remains for composting.
Moon in ♏ SCORPIO: transformational, magnetic, mysterious, hidden, sexual, erotic, secretive, musical, renewing, trust-worthy, loyal, supportive
Sun in ♒ AQUARIUS: humanitarian, collective, innovative, progressive, eccentric, detached, electric, friendly, generous, gregarious, unpredictable, aloof

I change perspective on _____

_____

_____

_____

_____

_____

_____

_____

My Tarot, Oracle, or Inspirational Card for Last Quarter Phase:_____

_____

_____

_____

_____

_____

_____

_____

_____

Balsamic   **February 8   04:54**   **Moon**   04°♑38'   **Natal House** _____
                                                Sun   19°♒38'   **Natal House** _____

How do I resolve the past Month and visualize, plan for up upcoming process? This is a pre-contemplative outlook. Seed is planted, released to develop next cycle/ germination begins.
Moon in ♑ CAPRICORN: authoritative, disciplined, realistic, responsible, practical, goal oriented, materialistic, successful, ambitious, professional, manifesting
Sun in ♒ AQUARIUS: humanitarian, collective, innovative, progressive, eccentric, detached, electric, friendly, generous, gregarious, unpredictable, aloof

I resolve/release and/or plan _____

_____

_____

_____

_____

_____

_____

_____

My Tarot, Oracle, or Inspirational Card for the First Quarter Phase: _____

_____

_____

_____

_____

_____

_____

_____

♒ Aquarius 2021

Ephemeris at Midnight UTC		Keywords for Natal Chart House
11-Feb	12°Aq42'	**1st House:** my body, my identity, myself, my appearance, my projected image, my soul-purpose, my initial approach to life, my interests, my sense of me
12-Feb	25°Aq58'	
13-Feb	08°Pi58'	**2nd House:** my talents, my resources, my values, my physical possessions, my money, my personal self-esteem, my sensuous enjoyment, myself worth
14-Feb	21°Pi42'	
15-Feb	04°Ar10'	**3rd House:** my adaptability, my communications, my siblings, my neighborhood, short journey, my active search for knowledge, learning, curiosity, thinking
16-Feb	16°Ar23'	
17-Feb	28°Ar24'	
18-Feb	10°Ta17'	**4th House:** my home, family, heritage, my privacy, my emotional life, feelings, eating habits, receptivity, my protective urges, vulnerability
19-Feb	22°Ta05'	
20-Feb	03°Ge55'	
21-Feb	15°Ge51'	**5th House:** my abilities, my creative ability, pregnancy, children, pleasures, will power, romance, merry making, vacation, affection, confidence
22-Feb	28°Ge00'	
23-Feb	10°Cn26'	**6th House:** my work conditions & habits, pets, my health, service offered, productivity, training, work skills, hygiene, clothing, nutrition & diet
24-Feb	23°Cn14'	
25-Feb	06°Le26'	
26-Feb	20°Le03'	**7th House:** agreements, contracts, partnerships, spouse, relationships, consultants, open enemies, receiving love, self-projection, social skills
27-Feb	04°Vi02'	
28-Feb	18°Vi21'	**8th House:** loyalty, partner's money & resources, taxes, inheritance, psychic & occult matters, transformation, shared values, sexual energy, investigations
1-Mar	02°Li51'	
2-Mar	17°Li27'	
3-Mar	02°Sc02'	**9th House:** wisdom, justice, law, exploration, faith, religious & spiritual pursuits, higher education, foreign travel, legal action, experimentation, seeking truth
4-Mar	16°Sc29'	
5-Mar	00°Sg45'	
6-Mar	14°Sg49'	**10th House:** accomplishments, authority, recognition, success, reputation, professional affairs, maturity, mastery, honor, self-fulfillment, public life
7-Mar	28°Sg39'	
8-Mar	12°Cp17'	**11th House:** groups & clubs, trends, friends, political awareness, emotional detachment, progressive thought, new technology & inventions, astrology
9-Mar	25°Cp44'	
10-Mar	08°Aq59'	
11-Mar	22°Aq03'	**12th House:** concern for others, self-sacrifice, psychological health, pre-natal imprinting, secret keeping, surrender, acceptance, spirituality
12-Mar	04°Pi57'	
13-Mar	17°Pi38'	

⬤ New	February 11 2021	19:05	Moon	23°♒16'	Natal House_____
			Sun	23°♒16'	

what am I open to for the upcoming cycle? What is entering my awareness? What does my intuition bring? This is a contemplative outlook. Seedling/Germination

Moon & Sun in ♒ AQUARIUS: humanitarian, collective, innovative, progressive, eccentric, detached, electric, friendly, generous, gregarious, unpredictable, aloof

I emerge with _____

_____

_____

_____

_____

_____

_____

my Tarot, Oracle, or Inspiration Card for Crescent Phase: _____

_____

_____

_____

_____

_____

_____

_____

_____

Crescent Moon   February 15   15:39   Moon 12°♈10'   Natal House _____
                                              Sun   27°♒10'   Natal House_____

What will I overcome that is worth letting go of? What are my resources? How do I prepare?
What change am I resisting? This is preparedness outlook. Sprout

Moon in ♈ARIES: assertive, courageous, independent, passionate, athletic, enthusiastic, active, aggressive, initiating, focused, forward, direct

Sun in ♒ AQUARIUS: humanitarian, collective, innovative, progressive, eccentric, detached, electric, friendly, generous, gregarious, unpredictable, aloof

I challenge myself to

_____

_____

_____

_____

_____

_____

_____

_____

my Tarot, Oracle, or Inspiration Card for Crescent Phase: _____

_____

_____

_____

_____

_____

_____

_____

First Quarter   February 19   18:47   Moon 01°♊20'   Natal House_____
                                              Sun   01°♓20'   Natal House_____

what steps will I take toward accomplishing my goals? How do I move forward in the next few days and/or long term? This is an action outlook. Root/Stem/Leaf – photosynthesis strengthens.
Moon in ♊ GEMINI: Clever, versatile, agile, curious, articulate, alert, conversational, adaptable, lighthearted, happy, quick-witted, cheerful
Sun in ♓ PISCES: spiritual, subtle, empathic, visionary, sensitive, psychic, vulnerable, intuitive, self-sacrificing, indulgent, loving, artistic

I take action on _____

_____

_____

_____

_____

_____

_____

_____

my Tarot, Oracle, or Inspirational Card for First Quarter Phase: _____

_____

_____

_____

_____

_____

_____

_____

Gibbous **February 23** **18:40 Moon 20°♋22'** **Natal House**_____
                                                      Sun   05°♓22' **Natal House**_____

How do I stay on track? What do I need to stay organized? What do I need to compromise if anything? This is a maintenance outlook. Buds appear and develop in size.

Moon in ♋ CANCER: nurturing, family oriented, watery, emotional, protective, psychic, domestic, sustaining, intuitive, sensitive, supportive, attached/connected

Sun in ♓ PISCES: spiritual, subtle, empathic, visionary, sensitive, psychic, vulnerable, intuitive, self-sacrificing, indulgent, loving, artistic

I develop structure with

_____

_____

_____

_____

_____

_____

_____

My Tarot, Oracle, or Inspirational Card for Gibbous Phase: _____

_____

_____

_____

_____

_____

_____

_____

Full Moon　　**February 27**　　　　**08:17 Moon 08°♍57'**　　　**Natal House**＿＿＿＿
　　　　　　　　　　　　　　　　　　　　Sun　　08°♓57'　　　**Natal House**＿＿＿＿

How do I see myself functioning in my world with my process? What does it look like within me and in my day to day world? This is a reflective outlook. Flower/Fruit

Moon in ♍ VIRGO: analytical, organized, efficient, health-conscious, conscientious, exacting, technical, healing, problem solving, scientific, time efficient

Sun in ♓ PISCES: spiritual, subtle, empathic, visionary, sensitive, psychic, vulnerable, intuitive, self- sacrificing, indulgent, loving, artistic

I reflect fulfillment with ＿＿＿＿＿＿＿＿＿＿＿＿＿＿＿＿＿＿＿＿＿＿＿

＿＿＿＿＿＿＿＿＿＿＿＿＿＿＿＿＿＿＿＿＿＿＿＿＿＿＿＿＿＿＿＿

＿＿＿＿＿＿＿＿＿＿＿＿＿＿＿＿＿＿＿＿＿＿＿＿＿＿＿＿＿＿＿＿

＿＿＿＿＿＿＿＿＿＿＿＿＿＿＿＿＿＿＿＿＿＿＿＿＿＿＿＿＿＿＿＿

＿＿＿＿＿＿＿＿＿＿＿＿＿＿＿＿＿＿＿＿＿＿＿＿＿＿＿＿＿＿＿＿

＿＿＿＿＿＿＿＿＿＿＿＿＿＿＿＿＿＿＿＿＿＿＿＿＿＿＿＿＿＿＿＿

＿＿＿＿＿＿＿＿＿＿＿＿＿＿＿＿＿＿＿＿＿＿＿＿＿＿＿＿＿＿＿＿

My Tarot, Oracle, or Inspirational Card for Full Moon Phase: ＿＿＿＿＿＿＿＿＿＿＿＿＿＿＿＿＿

＿＿＿＿＿＿＿＿＿＿＿＿＿＿＿＿＿＿＿＿＿＿＿＿＿＿＿＿＿＿＿＿

＿＿＿＿＿＿＿＿＿＿＿＿＿＿＿＿＿＿＿＿＿＿＿＿＿＿＿＿＿＿＿＿

＿＿＿＿＿＿＿＿＿＿＿＿＿＿＿＿＿＿＿＿＿＿＿＿＿＿＿＿＿＿＿＿

＿＿＿＿＿＿＿＿＿＿＿＿＿＿＿＿＿＿＿＿＿＿＿＿＿＿＿＿＿＿＿＿

＿＿＿＿＿＿＿＿＿＿＿＿＿＿＿＿＿＿＿＿＿＿＿＿＿＿＿＿＿＿＿＿

＿＿＿＿＿＿＿＿＿＿＿＿＿＿＿＿＿＿＿＿＿＿＿＿＿＿＿＿＿＿＿＿

◐ Disseminating   March 2   16:10   **Moon 27°♎17'**   **Natal House** _____
                                               Sun   12°♓17'   **Natal House** _____

How can I share my experiences? Where can I help others with my learning and experience?
This is a sharing outlook. First harvest.

Moon in ♎ LIBRA: cooperative, fair, considerate, artistic, tasteful, diplomatic, tactful, impartial,
refined, balanced, deliberate, soft-spoken, judgmental

Sun in ♓ PISCES: spiritual, subtle, empathic, visionary, sensitive, psychic, vulnerable, intuitive, self-
sacrificing, indulgent, loving, artistic

I share _____

_____

_____

_____

_____

_____

_____

_____

My Tarot, Oracle, or Inspirational Card for Disseminating Phase: _____

_____

_____

_____

_____

_____

_____

_____

_____

Last Quarter   **March 6**   **01:30**   **Moon 15°♐41'**   **Natal House** _____

                                                        Sun   15°♓41'   **Natal House** _____

How do I change or let go of the patterns that do not serve me and/or my community?
This is a reorienting outlook. Decay/Last Harvest and turning under of plant remains for composting.
Moon in ♐ SAGITTARIUS: expansive, philosophical, truth seeking, ethical, idealistic, optimistic, inspiring, wise, truth-seeking, motivational, truth speaking, honest
Sun in ♓ PISCES: spiritual, subtle, empathic, visionary, sensitive, psychic, vulnerable, intuitive, self-sacrificing, indulgent, loving, artistic

I change perspective on _____

_____

_____

_____

_____

_____

_____

_____

My Tarot, Oracle, or Inspirational Card for Last Quarter Phase:_____

_____

_____

_____

_____

_____

_____

_____

_____

Balsamic   March 9   15:25   Moon 04°♒16'   Natal House _____
                                                         Sun   19°♓16'   Natal House _____

How do I resolve the past Month and visualize, plan for up upcoming process? This is a pre-contemplative outlook. Seed is planted, released to develop next cycle/ germination begins.
Moon in ♒ AQUARIUS: humanitarian, collective, innovative, progressive, eccentric, detached, electric, friendly, generous, gregarious, unpredictable, aloof
Sun in ♓ PISCES: spiritual, subtle, empathic, visionary, sensitive, psychic, vulnerable, intuitive, self-sacrificing, indulgent, loving, artistic

I resolve/release and/or plan _____

_____

_____

_____

_____

_____

_____

_____

My Tarot, Oracle, or Inspirational Card for the Balsamic Phase:_____

_____

_____

_____

_____

_____

_____

_____

_____

♓ Pisces 2021

EPHEMERIS at Midnight UTC		Chart House keywords are nouns.
13-Mar	17°Pi38'	**1st House:** my body, my identity, myself, my appearance, my projected image, my soul-purpose, my initial approach to life, my interests, my sense of me
14-Mar	00°Ar08'	
15-Mar	12°Ar25'	
16-Mar	24°Ar32'	**2nd House:** my talents, my resources, my values, my physical possessions, my money, my personal self-esteem, my sensuous enjoyment, myself worth
17-Mar	06°Ta29'	
18-Mar	18°Ta19'	
19-Mar	00°Ge06'	**3rd House:** my adaptability, my communications, my siblings, my neighborhood, short journey, my active search for knowledge, learning, curiosity, thinking
Equinox 20-Mar	11°Ge54'	
21-Mar	23°Ge49'	
22-Mar	05°Cn56'	**4th House:** my home, family, heritage, my privacy, my emotional life, feelings, eating habits, receptivity, my protective urges, vulnerability
23-Mar	18°Cn20'	
24-Mar	01°Le06'	
25-Mar	14°Le19'	**5th House:** my abilities, my creative ability, pregnancy, children, pleasures, will power, romance, merry making, vacation, affection, confidence
26-Mar	28°Le00'	
27-Mar	12°Vi09'	
28-Mar	26°Vi41'	**6th House:** my work conditions & habits, pets, my health, service offered, productivity, training, work skills, hygiene, clothing, nutrition & diet
29-Mar	11°Li32'	
30-Mar	26°Li31'	
31-Mar	11°Sc30'	**7th House:** agreements, contracts, partnerships, spouse, relationships, consultants, open enemies, receiving love, self-projection, social skills
1-Apr	26°Sc20'	
2-Apr	10°Sg55'	**8th House:** loyalty, partner's money & resources, taxes, inheritance, psychic & occult matters, transformation, shared values, sexual energy, investigations
3-Apr	25°Sg11'	
4-Apr	09°Cp07'	
5-Apr	22°Cp43'	**9th House:** wisdom, justice, law, exploration, faith, religious & spiritual pursuits, higher education, foreign travel, legal action, experimentation, seeking truth
6-Apr	06°Aq01'	
7-Apr	19°Aq03'	
8-Apr	01°Pi50'	**10th House:** accomplishments, authority, recognition, success, reputation, professional affairs, maturity, mastery, honor, self-fulfillment, public life
9-Apr	14°Pi25'	
10-Apr	26°Pi49'	
11-Apr	09°Ar03'	**11th House:** groups & clubs, trends, friends, political awareness, emotional detachment, progressive thought, new technology & inventions, astrology
12-Apr	21°Ar09'	
		12th House: concern for others, self-sacrifice, psychological health, pre-natal imprinting, secret keeping, surrender, acceptance, spirituality

New   **March 13**   **10:21**   **Moon 23°♓03'**   **Natal House_____**

                                                            Sun   23°♓03'   **Natal House_____**

What am I open to for the upcoming cycle? What is entering my awareness? What does my intuition bring? This is a contemplative outlook. Seedling/Germination

Moon & Sun in ♓ PISCES: spiritual, subtle, empathic, visionary, sensitive, psychic, vulnerable, intuitive, self-sacrificing, indulgent, loving, artistic

I emerge with

_____

_____

_____

_____

_____

_____

_____

_____

My Tarot, Oracle, or Inspirational Card for the New Moon Phase: _____

_____

_____

_____

_____

_____

_____

_____

Crescent   March 17   11:20   Moon 12°♉05'   Natal House_____

                                                    Sun   27°♓05'   Natal House_____

What will I overcome that is worth letting go of? What are my resources? How do I prepare? What change am I resisting? This is preparedness outlook. Sprout

Moon in ♉ TAURUS: sensual, physical, reliable, consistent, resourceful, deliberate, passive, practical, sensual, financial, valued, comfortable

Sun in ♓ PISCES: spiritual, subtle, empathic, visionary, sensitive, psychic, vulnerable, intuitive, self-sacrificing, indulgent, loving, artistic

I challenge myself to

_____

_____

_____

_____

_____

_____

_____

_____

My Tarot, Oracle, or Inspiration Card for Crescent Phase: _____

_____

_____

_____

_____

_____

_____

_____

First Quarter   March 21   14:40   Moon 01°♋12'   Natal House_____
                                          Sun   01°♈'12'   Natal House_____

What are my steps toward accomplishing my goals? How do I move forward in the next few days and/or long term? This is an action outlook. Root/Stem/Leaf – photosynthesis strengthens.

Moon in ♋ CANCER: nurturing, family oriented, watery, emotional, protective, psychic, domestic, sustaining, intuitive, sensitive, supportive, attached/connected

Sun in ♈ ARIES: assertive, courageous, independent, passionate, athletic, enthusiastic, active, aggressive, initiating, focused, forward, direct

I take action on

_____

_____

_____

_____

_____

_____

_____

My Tarot, Oracle, or Inspirational Card for First Quarter Phase: _____

_____

_____

_____

_____

_____

_____

_____

Gibbous   **March 25 2021**   **10:00 Moon 19°♌58'**   **Natal House**_____

                                         Sun   04°♈58'   **Natal House**_____

How do I stay on track? What do I need to stay organized? What do I need to compromise if anything?
This is a maintenance outlook. Buds appear and develop in size.

Moon in ♌ LEO: self-confident, dignified, generous, playful, dramatic, courageous, caring, radiant, romantic, loving, self-centered/focused, strong hearted, brave

Sun in ♈ ARIES: assertive, courageous, independent, passionate, athletic, enthusiastic, active, aggressive, initiating, focused, forward, direct

I develop structure with
_____

_____

_____

_____

_____

_____

_____

_____

My Tarot, Oracle, or Inspirational Card for Gibbous Phase: _____

_____

_____

_____

_____

_____

_____

_____

49

Full   March 28   18:48   Moon 08°♎18'   Natal House_____
                              Sun 08°♈18'   Natal House_____

How do I see myself functioning in my world with my process? What does it look like within me and in my day to day world? This is a reflective outlook. Flower/Fruit

Moon in ♎ LIBRA: cooperative, fair, considerate, artistic, tasteful, diplomatic, tactful, impartial, refined, balanced, deliberate, soft-spoken, judgmental

Sun in ♈ ARIES: assertive, courageous, independent, passionate, athletic, enthusiastic, active, aggressive, initiating, focused, forward, direct

I reflect fulfillment with

_____

_____

_____

_____

_____

_____

_____

My Tarot, Oracle, or Inspirational Card for Full Moon Phase: _____

_____

_____

_____

_____

_____

_____

_____

_____

◐ **Disseminating**   April 1   00:14 Moon 26°♏29'   Natal House _____
                                                Sun   11°♈29'   Natal House _____

How can I share my experiences? Where can I help others with my learning and experience?
this is a sharing outlook. First harvest.

Moon in ♏ SCORPIO: transformational, magnetic, mysterious, hidden, sexual, erotic, secretive, musical, renewing, trust-worthy, loyal, supportive

Sun in ♈ ARIES: assertive, courageous, independent, passionate, athletic, enthusiastic, active, aggressive, initiating, focused, forward, direct

I share

_____

_____

_____

_____

_____

_____

_____

my Tarot, Oracle, or Inspirational Card for Disseminating Phase:_____

_____

_____

_____

_____

_____

_____

Last Quarter   April 4   10:02   Moon 14°♑51'   Natal House _____

                                                  Sun   14°♈51'   Natal House _____

How do I change or let go of the patterns that do not serve me and/or my community?
This is a reorienting outlook. Decay/Last Harvest and turning under of plant remains for composting.
Moon in ♑ CAPRICORN: authoritative, disciplined, realistic, responsible, practical, goal oriented, materialistic, successful, ambitious, professional, manifesting
Sun in ♈ ARIES: assertive, courageous, independent, passionate, athletic, enthusiastic, active, aggressive, initiating, focused, forward, direct

I change perspective on
_____

_____

_____

_____

_____

_____

_____

_____

My Tarot, Oracle, or Inspirational Card for Last Quarter Phase:_____

_____

_____

_____

_____

_____

_____

_____

_____

_____

Balsamic   **April 8**   **03:08 Moon 03°♓30'**   **Natal House** _____
                                  Sun   18°♈30'   **Natal House** _____

How do I resolve the past Month and visualize, plan for up upcoming process? This is a pre-contemplative outlook. Seed is planted, released to develop next cycle/ germination begins.

Moon in ♓ PISCES: spiritual, subtle, empathic, visionary, sensitive, psychic, vulnerable, intuitive, self-sacrificing, indulgent, loving, artistic

Sun in ♈ ARIES: assertive, courageous, independent, passionate, athletic, enthusiastic, active, aggressive, initiating, focused, forward, direct

I resolve/release and/or plan

_____

_____

_____

_____

_____

_____

_____

My Tarot, Oracle, or Inspirational Card for the Balsamic Phase:_____

_____

_____

_____

_____

_____

_____

_____

♈ Aries 2021

Ephemeris at Midnight UTC	
12-Apr	21°Ar09'
13-Apr	03°Ta06'
14-Apr	14°Ta58'
15-Apr	26°Ta46'
16-Apr	08°Ge32'
17-Apr	20°Ge21'
18-Apr	02°Cn17'
19-Apr	14°Cn23'
20-Apr	26°Cn45'
21-Apr	09°Le28'
22-Apr	22°Le36'
23-Apr	06°Vi12'
24-Apr	20°Vi17'
25-Apr	04°Li49'
26-Apr	19°Li43'
27-Apr	04°Sc52'
28-Apr	20°Sc04'
29-Apr	05°Sg12'
30-Apr	20°Sg05'
1-May	04°Cp38'
2-May	18°Cp47'
3-May	02°Aq32'
4-May	15°Aq52'
5-May	28°Aq51'
6-May	11°Pi31'
7-May	23°Pi56'
8-May	06°Ar08'
9-May	18°Ar11'
10-May	00°Ta06'
11-May	11°Ta57'
12-May	23°Ta45'

Chart House keywords are nouns.

1st House: my body, my identity, myself, my appearance, my projected image, my soul-purpose, my initial approach to life, my interests, my sense of me

2nd House: my talents, my resources, my values, my physical possessions, my money, my personal self-esteem, my sensuous enjoyment, myself worth

3rd House: my adaptability, my communications, my siblings, my neighborhood, short journey, my active search for knowledge, learning, curiosity, thinking

4th House: my home, family, heritage, my privacy, my emotional life, feelings, eating habits, receptivity, my protective urges, vulnerability

5th House: my abilities, my creative ability, pregnancy, children, pleasures, will power, romance, merry making, vacation, affection, confidence

6th House: my work conditions & habits, pets, my health, service offered, productivity, training, work skills, hygiene, clothing, nutrition & diet

7th House: agreements, contracts, partnerships, spouse, relationships, consultants, open enemies, receiving love, self-projection, social skills

8th House: loyalty, partner's money & resources, taxes, inheritance, psychic & occult matters, transformation, shared values, sexual energy, investigations

9th House: wisdom, justice, law, exploration, faith, religious & spiritual pursuits, higher education, foreign travel, legal action, experimentation, seeking truth

10th House: accomplishments, authority, recognition, success, reputation, professional affairs, maturity, mastery, honor, self-fulfillment, public life

11th House: groups & clubs, trends, friends, political awareness, emotional detachment, progressive thought, new technology & inventions, astrology

12th House: concern for others, self-sacrifice, psychological health, pre-natal imprinting, secret keeping, surrender, acceptance, spirituality

New Moon   **April 12**   **02:30**   **Moon 22°♈24'**   **Natal House_____**
                                                       Sun   22°♈24'

What am I open to for the upcoming cycle? What is entering my awareness? What does my intuition bring? This is a contemplative outlook. Seedling/Germination

Moon & Sun in ♈ ARIES: assertive, courageous, independent, passionate, athletic, enthusiastic, active, aggressive, initiating, focused, forward, direct

I emerge with _____

_____

_____

_____

_____

_____

My Tarot, Oracle, or Inspirational Card for New Moon Phase: _____

_____

_____

_____

_____

_____

_____

_____

Crescent   **April 16**   **05:57**   **Moon 11°Ⅱ28'**   **Natal House**_____

                                                                  Sun   26°♈28'   **Natal House**_____

What will I overcome that is worth letting go of? What are my resources? How do I prepare? What change am I resisting? This is preparedness outlook. Sprout

Moon in Ⅱ GEMINI: Clever, versatile, agile, curious, articulate, alert, conversational, adaptable, lighthearted, happy, quick-witted, cheerful

Sun in ♈ ARIES: assertive, courageous, independent, passionate, athletic, enthusiastic, active, aggressive, initiating, focused, forward, direct

I challenge myself to

_____

_____

_____

_____

_____

_____

_____

_____

My Tarot, Oracle, or Inspiration Card for Crescent Phase: _____

_____

_____

_____

_____

_____

_____

First Quarter   **April 20**   **06:58**   **Moon** 00°♌25'   **Natal House**_____

                                                                        Sun   00°♉25'   **Natal House**_____

What steps will I take toward accomplishing my goals? How do I move forward in the next few days and/or long term? This is an action outlook. Root/Stem/Leaf – photosynthesis strengthens.

Moon in ♌ LEO: self-confident, dignified, generous, playful, dramatic, courageous, caring, radiant, romantic, loving, self-centered/focused, strong hearted, brave

Sun in ♉ TAURUS: sensual, physical, reliable, consistent, resourceful, deliberate, passive, practical, sensual, financial, valued, comfortable

I take action on
_____

_____

_____

_____

_____

_____

_____

My Tarot, Oracle, or Inspirational Card for First Quarter Phase:_____

_____

_____

_____

_____

_____

_____

_____

Gibbous   **April 23**   **21:44**   **Moon 18° ♍ 56'**   **Natal House_____**

                                                       Sun   03° ♉ 56'   **Natal House_____**

How do I stay on track? What do I need to stay organized? What do I need to compromise if anything? This is a maintenance outlook. Buds appear and develop in size.

Moon in ♍ VIRGO: analytical, organized, efficient, health-conscious, conscientious, exacting, technical, healing, problem solving, scientific, time efficient

Sun in ♉ TAURUS: sensual, physical, reliable, consistent, resourceful, deliberate, passive, practical, sensual, financial, valued, comfortable

I develop structure with
_____

_____

_____

_____

_____

_____

_____

_____

My Tarot, Oracle, or Inspirational Card for Gibbous Phase:_____

_____

_____

_____

_____

_____

_____

Full   **April 27**   **03:31**   **Moon 07° ♏ 06'**   **Natal House**_____

                                                              Sun   07° ♉ 06'   **Natal House**_____

How do I see myself functioning in my world with my process? What does it look like within me and in my day to day world? This is a reflective outlook. Flower/Fruit

Moon in ♏ SCORPIO: transformational, magnetic, mysterious, hidden, sexual, erotic, secretive, musical, renewing, trust-worthy, loyal, supportive

Sun in ♉ TAURUS: sensual, physical, reliable, consistent, resourceful, deliberate, passive, practical, sensual, financial, valued, comfortable

I reflect fulfillment with _____

_____

_____

_____

_____

_____

_____

My Tarot, Oracle, or Inspirational Card for Full Moon Phase: _____

_____

_____

_____

_____

_____

_____

◐ **Disseminating**   **April 30**   **08:22**   **Moon 25°♐12'**   **Natal House _____**

                                                Sun   10°♉12'   **Natal House _____**

how can I share my experiences? Where can I help others with my learning and experience? this is a sharing outlook. First harvest.

moon in ♐ SAGITTARIUS: expansive, philosophical, truth seeking, ethical, idealistic, optimistic, inspiring, wise, truth-seeking, motivational, truth speaking, honest

sun in ♉ TAURUS: sensual, physical, reliable, consistent, resourceful, deliberate, passive, practical, sensual, financial, valued, comfortable

I share

_____

_____

_____

_____

_____

_____

_____

My Tarot, Oracle, or Inspirational Card for Disseminating Phase: _____

_____

_____

_____

_____

_____

_____

_____

_____

Last Quarter   May 3   19:49   Moon 13°♒35'   Natal House _____
                                  Sun   13°♉35'   Natal House _____

How do I change or let go of the patterns that do not serve me and/or my community?
This is a reorienting outlook. Decay/Last Harvest and turning under of plant remains for composting.
Moon in ♒ AQUARIUS: humanitarian, collective, innovative, progressive, eccentric, detached, electric, friendly, generous, gregarious, unpredictable, aloof
Sun in ♉ TAURUS: sensual, physical, reliable, consistent, resourceful, deliberate, passive, practical, sensual, financial, valued, comfortable

I change perspective on
_____

_____

_____

_____

_____

_____

_____

_____

My Tarot, Oracle, or Inspirational Card for Last Quarter Phase: _____

_____

_____

_____

_____

_____

_____

_____

_____

Balsamic   **May 7**   **16:27**   **Moon 02°♈19'**   **Natal House** _____
                                                          Sun   17°♉19'   **Natal House** _____

How do I resolve the past Month and visualize, plan for up upcoming process? This is a pre-contemplative outlook. Seed is planted, released to develop next cycle/ germination begins.
Moon in ♈ ARIES: assertive, courageous, independent, passionate, athletic, enthusiastic, active, aggressive, initiating, focused, forward, direct
Sun in ♉ TAURUS: sensual, physical, reliable, consistent, resourceful, deliberate, passive, practical, sensual, financial, valued, comfortable

I resolve/release and/or plan _____

_____

_____

_____

_____

_____

_____

_____

My Tarot, Oracle, or Inspirational Card for the Balsamic Phase: _____

_____

_____

_____

_____

_____

_____

_____

♉ Taurus 2021 Total Lunar Eclipse

EPHEMERIS at Midnight UTC		Chart House keywords are nouns. (Signs are adjectives.)
11-May	11°Ta57'	**1st House:** my body, my identity, myself, my appearance, my projected image, my soul-purpose, my initial approach to life, my interests, my sense of me
12-May	23°Ta45'	
13-May	05°Ge32'	
14-May	17°Ge21'	**2nd House:** my talents, my resources, my values, my physical possessions, my money, my personal self-esteem, my sensuous enjoyment, myself worth
15-May	29°Ge15'	
16-May	11°Cn15'	
17-May	23°Cn26'	**3rd House:** my adaptability, my communications, my siblings, my neighborhood, short journey, my active search for knowledge, learning, curiosity, thinking
18-May	05°Le51'	
19-May	18°Le35'	
20-May	01°Vi39'	**4th House:** my home, family, heritage, my privacy, my emotional life, feelings, eating habits, receptivity, my protective urges, vulnerability
21-May	15°Vi08'	
22-May	29°Vi03'	**5th House:** my abilities, my creative ability, pregnancy, children, pleasures, will power, romance, merry making, vacation, affection, confidence
23-May	13°Li24'	
24-May	28°Li07'	
25-May	13°Sc08'	**6th House:** my work conditions & habits, pets, my health, service offered, productivity, training, work skills, hygiene, clothing, nutrition & diet
26-May	28°Sc19'	
27-May	13°Sg29'	**7th House:** agreements, contracts, partnerships, spouse, relationships, consultants, open enemies, receiving love, self-projection, social skills
28-May	28°Sg31'	
29-May	13°Cp15'	
30-May	27°Cp36'	**8th House:** loyalty, partner's money & resources, taxes, inheritance, psychic & occult matters, transformation, shared values, sexual energy, investigations
31-May	11°Aq31'	
1-Jun	24°Aq59'	**9th House:** wisdom, justice, law, exploration, faith, religious & spiritual pursuits, higher education, foreign travel, legal action, experimentation, seeking truth
2-Jun	08°Pi02'	
3-Jun	20°Pi42'	
4-Jun	03°Ar04'	**10th House:** accomplishments, authority, recognition, success, reputation, professional affairs, maturity, mastery, honor, self-fulfillment, public life
5-Jun	15°Ar11'	
6-Jun	27°Ar08'	**11th House:** groups & clubs, trends, friends, political awareness, emotional detachment, progressive thought, new technology & inventions, astrology
7-Jun	08°Ta59'	
8-Jun	20°Ta46'	
9-Jun	02°Ge33'	**12th House:** concern for others, self-sacrifice, psychological health, pre-natal imprinting, secret keeping, surrender, acceptance, spirituality
10-Jun	14°Ge23'	

New   **May 11**   **18:59**   **Moon 21°♉17'**   **Natal House_____**
                                              Sun   21°♉17'

What am I open to for the upcoming cycle? What is entering my awareness? What does my intuition bring? This is a contemplative outlook. Seedling/Germination

Moon & Sun in ♉ TAURUS: sensual, physical, reliable, consistent, resourceful, deliberate, passive, practical, sensual, financial, valued, comfortable

I emerge with

_____

_____

_____

_____

_____

_____

_____

My Tarot, Oracle, or Inspirational Card for New Moon Phase: _____

_____

_____

_____

_____

_____

_____

_____

_____

_____

Crescent   **May 15**   **22:03**   **Moon 10°♋16'**   **Natal House**_____

                                          Sun   **25°♉16'**   **Natal House**_____

What will I overcome that is worth letting go of? What are my resources? How do I prepare? What change am I resisting? This is preparedness outlook. Sprout

Moon in ♋ CANCER: nurturing, family oriented, watery, emotional, protective, psychic, domestic, sustaining, intuitive, sensitive, supportive, attached/connected

Sun in ♉ TAURUS: sensual, physical, reliable, consistent, resourceful, deliberate, passive, practical, sensual, financial, valued, comfortable

I challenge myself to _____

_____

_____

_____

_____

_____

_____

My Tarot, Oracle, or Inspiration Card for Crescent Phase: _____

_____

_____

_____

_____

_____

_____

First Quarter   **May 19**   **19:12**   **Moon 29° ♌ 01'**   **Natal House_____**
                                                        Sun   29° ♉ 01'   **Natal House_____**

What steps will I take toward accomplishing my goals? How do I move forward in the next few days and/or long term? This is an action outlook. Root/Stem/Leaf – photosynthesis strengthens.

Moon in ♌ LEO: self-confident, dignified, generous, playful, dramatic, courageous, caring, radiant, romantic, loving, self-centered/focused, strong hearted, brave

Sun in ♉ TAURUS: sensual, physical, reliable, consistent, resourceful, deliberate, passive, practical, sensual, financial, valued, comfortable

I take action on _____

_____

_____

_____

_____

_____

_____

_____

My Tarot, Oracle, or Inspirational Card for First Quarter Phase: _____

_____

_____

_____

_____

_____

_____

_____

Gibbous **May 23** **06:29** **Moon 17°♎21'** **Natal House_____**

Sun 02°♊21' **Natal House_____**

How do I stay on track? What do I need to stay organized? What do I need to compromise if anything? This is a maintenance outlook. Buds appear and develop in size.

Moon in ♎ LIBRA: cooperative, fair, considerate, artistic, tasteful, diplomatic, tactful, impartial, refined, balanced, deliberate, soft-spoken, judgmental

Sun in ♊ GEMINI: Clever, versatile, agile, curious, articulate, alert, conversational, adaptable, lighthearted, happy, quick-witted, cheerful

I develop structure with _____

_____

_____

_____

_____

_____

_____

_____

My Tarot, Oracle, or Inspirational Card for Gibbous Phase:_____

_____

_____

_____

_____

_____

_____

_____

Total Lunar Eclipse

Full	May 26	11:13	Moon 05°♐25'	Natal House_____
			Sun 05°♊25'	Natal House_____

How do I see myself functioning in my world with my process? What does it look like within me and in my day to day world? This is a reflective outlook. Flower/Fruit

Moon in ♐ SAGITTARIUS: expansive, philosophical, truth seeking, ethical, idealistic, optimistic, inspiring, wise, truth-seeking, motivational, truth speaking, honest

Sun in ♊ GEMINI: Clever, versatile, agile, curious, articulate, alert, conversational, adaptable, lighthearted, happy, quick-witted, cheerful

I reflect fulfillment with

_____

_____

_____

_____

_____

_____

_____

My Tarot, Oracle, or Inspirational Card for Full Moon Phase: _____

_____

_____

_____

_____

_____

_____

◐ Disseminating   May 29   17:07   Moon 23°♑32'   Natal House _____
                                          Sun   08°♊32'   Natal House _____

How can I share my experiences? Where can I help others with my learning and experience? this is a sharing outlook. First harvest.

Moon in ♑ CAPRICORN: authoritative, disciplined, realistic, responsible, practical, goal oriented, materialistic, successful, ambitious, professional, manifesting

Sun in ♊ GEMINI: Clever, versatile, agile, curious, articulate, alert, conversational, adaptable, lighthearted, happy, quick-witted, cheerful

I share _____

_____

_____

_____

_____

_____

_____

_____

my Tarot, Oracle, or Inspirational Card for Disseminating Phase: _____

_____

_____

_____

_____

_____

_____

_____

Last Quarter   June 2   07:24   Moon 11°♓59'   Natal House _____
                                                     Sun   11°♊59'   Natal House _____

How do I change or let go of the patterns that do not serve me and/or my community?
This is a reorienting outlook. Decay/Last Harvest and turning under of plant remains for composting.
Moon in ♓ PISCES: spiritual, subtle, empathic, visionary, sensitive, psychic, vulnerable, intuitive, self-sacrificing, indulgent, loving, artistic
Sun in ♊ GEMINI: Clever, versatile, agile, curious, articulate, alert, conversational, adaptable, lighthearted, happy, quick-witted, cheerful

I change perspective on
_____

_____

_____

_____

_____

_____

_____

_____

My Tarot, Oracle, or Inspirational Card for Last Quarter Phase: _____

_____

_____

_____

_____

_____

_____

_____

Balsamic **June 6** **07:25**   **Moon 00°♉49'**   **Natal House** _____
                                          Sun **15°♊49'**   **Natal House** _____

How do I resolve the past Month and visualize, plan for up upcoming process? This is a pre-contemplative outlook. Seed is planted, released to develop next cycle/ germination begins.

Moon in ♉ TAURUS: sensual, physical, reliable, consistent, resourceful, deliberate, passive, practical, sensual, financial, valued, comfortable

Sun in ♊ GEMINI: Clever, versatile, agile, curious, articulate, alert, conversational, adaptable, lighthearted, happy, quick-witted, cheerful

I resolve/release and/or plan

_____

_____

_____

_____

_____

_____

_____

My Tarot, Oracle, or Inspirational Card for the Balsamic Phase:_____

_____

_____

_____

_____

_____

_____

_____

♊ Gemini 2021 Solar Annular Eclipse

EPHEMERIS at Midnight UTC		Chart House keywords are nouns.
10-Jun	14°Ge23'	**1st House:** my body, my identity, myself, my appearance, my projected image, my soul-purpose, my initial approach to life, my interests, my sense of me
11-Jun	26°Ge18'	
12-Jun	08°Cn21'	
13-Jun	20°Cn32'	**2nd House:** my talents, my resources, my values, my physical possessions, my money, my personal self-esteem, my sensuous enjoyment, myself worth
14-Jun	02°Le55'	
15-Jun	15°Le30'	
16-Jun	28°Le21'	**3rd House:** my adaptability, my communications, my siblings, my neighborhood, short journey, my active search for knowledge, learning, curiosity, thinking
17-Jun	11°Vi29'	
18-Jun	24°Vi55'	
19-Jun	08°Li42'	**4th House:** my home, family, heritage, my privacy, my emotional life, feelings, eating habits, receptivity, my protective urges, vulnerability
20-Jun	22°Li50'	
Solstice 21-Jun	07°Sc16'	**5th House:** my abilities, my creative ability, pregnancy, children, pleasures, will power, romance, merry making, vacation, affection, confidence
22-Jun	21°Sc59'	
23-Jun	06°Sg53'	
24-Jun	21°Sg51'	**6th House:** my work conditions & habits, pets, my health, service offered, productivity, training, work skills, hygiene, clothing, nutrition & diet
25-Jun	06°Cp45'	
26-Jun	21°Cp28'	**7th House:** agreements, contracts, partnerships, spouse, relationships, consultants, open enemies, receiving love, self-projection, social skills
27-Jun	05°Aq52'	
28-Jun	19°Aq52'	
29-Jun	03°Pi26'	**8th House:** loyalty, partner's money & resources, taxes, inheritance, psychic & occult matters, transformation, shared values, sexual energy, investigations
30-Jun	16°Pi33'	
1-Jul	29°Pi17'	**9th House:** wisdom, justice, law, exploration, faith, religious & spiritual pursuits, higher education, foreign travel, legal action, experimentation, seeking truth
2-Jul	11°Ar40'	
3-Jul	23°Ar47'	
4-Jul	05°Ta42'	**10th House:** accomplishments, authority, recognition, success, reputation, professional affairs, maturity, mastery, honor, self-fulfillment, public life
5-Jul	17°Ta31'	
6-Jul	29°Ta18'	
7-Jul	11°Ge08'	**11th House:** groups & clubs, trends, friends, political awareness, emotional detachment, progressive thought, new technology & inventions, astrology
8-Jul	23°Ge03'	
9-Jul	05°Cn07'	**12th House:** concern for others, self-sacrifice, psychological health, pre-natal imprinting, secret keeping, surrender, acceptance, spirituality
10-Jul	17°Cn22'	

Solar Annular Eclipse

New	June 10	10:52	Moon	19°Ⅱ47'	Natal House_____
			Sun	19°Ⅱ47'	

What am I open to for the upcoming cycle? What is entering my awareness? What does my intuition bring? This is a contemplative outlook. Seedling/Germination

Moon & Sun in Ⅱ GEMINI: Clever, versatile, agile, curious, articulate, alert, conversational, adaptable, lighthearted, happy, quick-witted, cheerful

I emerge with _____

_____

_____

_____

_____

_____

_____

My Tarot, Oracle, or Inspirational Card for New Moon Phase: _____

_____

_____

_____

_____

_____

_____

_____

_____

Crescent   June 14   10:53   Moon 08°♌36'   Natal House_____
                                        Sun   23°♊36'   Natal House_____

What will I overcome that is worth letting go of? What are my resources? How do I prepare? What change am I resisting? This is preparedness outlook. Sprout

Moon in ♌ LEO: self-confident, dignified, generous, playful, dramatic, courageous, caring, radiant, romantic, loving, self-centered/focused, strong hearted, brave

Sun in ♊ GEMINI: Clever, versatile, agile, curious, articulate, alert, conversational, adaptable, lighthearted, happy, quick-witted, cheerful

I challenge myself to

_____

_____

_____

_____

_____

_____

_____

_____

My Tarot, Oracle, or Inspiration Card for Crescent Phase: _____

_____

_____

_____

_____

_____

_____

_____

First Quarter   June 18   03:54   Moon 27°♍09'   Natal House_____

Sun   27°♊09'   Natal House_____

What steps will I take toward accomplishing my goals? How do I move forward in the next few days and/or long term? This is an action outlook. Root/Stem/Leaf – photosynthesis strengthens.

Moon in ♍ VIRGO: analytical, organized, efficient, health-conscious, conscientious, exacting, technical, healing, problem solving, scientific, time efficient

Sun in ♊ GEMINI: Clever, versatile, agile, curious, articulate, alert, conversational, adaptable, lighthearted, happy, quick-witted, cheerful

I take action on _____

_____

_____

_____

_____

_____

_____

_____

My Tarot, Oracle, or Inspirational Card for First Quarter Phase: _____

_____

_____

_____

_____

_____

_____

_____

Gibbous   **June 21**   **13:16**   **Moon 15° ♏ 23'**   **Natal House_____**
                                                   Sun   00° ♋ 23'   **Natal House_____**

How do I stay on track? What do I need to stay organized? What do I need to compromise if anything? This is a maintenance outlook. Buds appear and develop in size.

Moon in ♏ SCORPIO: transformational, magnetic, mysterious, hidden, sexual, erotic, secretive, musical, renewing, trust-worthy, loyal, supportive

Sun in ♋ CANCER: nurturing, family oriented, watery, emotional, protective, psychic, domestic, sustaining, intuitive, sensitive, supportive, attached/connected

I develop structure with

_____

_____

_____

_____

_____

_____

_____

My Tarot, Oracle, or Inspirational Card for Gibbous Phase:_____

_____

_____

_____

_____

_____

_____

_____

◯ **Full**   **June 24**   **18:39**   **Moon 03°♑27'**   **Natal House_____**
                                              Sun   03°♋27'   **Natal House_____**

How do I see myself functioning in my world with my process? What does it look like within me and in my day to day world? This is a reflective outlook. Flower/Fruit

Moon in ♑ CAPRICORN: authoritative, disciplined, realistic, responsible, practical, goal oriented, materialistic, successful, ambitious, professional, manifesting

Sun in ♋ CANCER: nurturing, family oriented, watery, emotional, protective, psychic, domestic, sustaining, intuitive, sensitive, supportive, attached/connected

I reflect fulfillment with

_____

_____

_____

_____

_____

_____

_____

My Tarot, Oracle, or Inspirational Card for Full Moon Phase:_____

_____

_____

_____

_____

_____

_____

_____

_____

◗ Disseminating   June 28   03:06 Moon 21°♒39'   Natal House _____
                                    Sun   06°♋39'   Natal House _____

How can I share my experiences? Where can I help others with my learning and experience?
This is a sharing outlook. First harvest.

Moon in ♒ AQUARIUS: humanitarian, collective, innovative, progressive, eccentric, detached, electric, friendly, generous, gregarious, unpredictable, aloof

Sun in ♋ CANCER: nurturing, family oriented, watery, emotional, protective, psychic, domestic, sustaining, intuitive, sensitive, supportive, attached/connected

I share _____

_____

_____

_____

_____

_____

_____

My Tarot, Oracle, or Inspirational Card for Disseminating Phase:_____

_____

_____

_____

_____

_____

_____

_____

_____

Last Quarter **July 1** **21:10** **Moon** 10°♈14' **Natal House** _____

Sun 10°♋14' **Natal House** _____

How do I change or let go of the patterns that do not serve me and/or my community?

This is a reorienting outlook. Decay/Last Harvest and turning under of plant remains for composting.

Moon in ♈ ARIES: assertive, courageous, independent, passionate, athletic, enthusiastic, active, aggressive, initiating, focused, forward, direct

Sun in ♋ CANCER: nurturing, family oriented, watery, emotional, protective, psychic, domestic, sustaining, intuitive, sensitive, supportive, attached/connected

I change perspective on _____

_____

_____

_____

_____

_____

_____

_____

My Tarot, Oracle, or Inspirational Card for Last Quarter Phase: _____

_____

_____

_____

_____

_____

_____

_____

Balsamic   July 5   23:39   Moon 29° ♉ 08'   Natal House _____

Sun   14° ♋ 08'   Natal House _____

How do I resolve the past Month and visualize, plan for up upcoming process? This is a pre-contemplative outlook. Seed is planted, released to develop next cycle/ germination begins.

Moon in ♉ TAURUS: sensual, physical, reliable, consistent, resourceful, deliberate, passive, practical, sensual, financial, valued, comfortable

Sun in ♋ CANCER: nurturing, family oriented, watery, emotional, protective, psychic, domestic, sustaining, intuitive, sensitive, supportive, attached/connected

I resolve/release and/or plan _____

_____

_____

_____

_____

_____

_____

My Tarot, Oracle, or Inspirational Card for the Balsamic Phase: _____

_____

_____

_____

_____

_____

_____

_____

♋ Cancer 2021

EPHEMERIS at Midnight UTC	
10-Jul	17°Cn22'
11-Jul	29°Cn49'
12-Jul	12°Le29'
13-Jul	25°Le22'
14-Jul	08°Vi29'
15-Jul	21°Vi49'
16-Jul	05°Li22'
17-Jul	19°Li09'
18-Jul	03°Sc08'
19-Jul	17°Sc20'
20-Jul	01°Sg43'
21-Jul	16°Sg15'
22-Jul	00°Cp50'
23-Jul	15°Cp25'
24-Jul	29°Cp52'
25-Jul	14°Aq05'
26-Jul	28°Aq00'
27-Jul	11°Pi32'
28-Jul	24°Pi39'
29-Jul	07°Ar24'
30-Jul	19°Ar48'
31-Jul	01°Ta56'
1-Aug	13°Ta52'
2-Aug	25°Ta41'
3-Aug	07°Ge29'
4-Aug	19°Ge21'
5-Aug	01°Cn22'
6-Aug	13°Cn34'
7-Aug	26°Cn02'
8-Aug	08°Le46'

Chart House keywords are nouns.
Sign keywords are adjectives.

1st House: my body, my identity, myself, my appearance, my projected image, my soul-purpose, my initial approach to life, my interests, my sense of me

2nd House: my talents, my resources, my values, my physical possessions, my money, my personal self-esteem, my sensuous enjoyment, myself worth

3rd House: my adaptability, my communications, my siblings, my neighborhood, short journey, my active search for knowledge, learning, curiosity, thinking

4th House: my home, family, heritage, my privacy, my emotional life, feelings, eating habits, receptivity, my protective urges, vulnerability

5th House: my abilities, my creative ability, pregnancy, children, pleasures, will power, romance, merry making, vacation, affection, confidence

6th House: my work conditions & habits, pets, my health, service offered, productivity, training, work skills, hygiene, clothing, nutrition & diet

7th House: agreements, contracts, partnerships, spouse, relationships, consultants, open enemies, receiving love, self-projection, social skills

8th House: loyalty, partner's money & resources, taxes, inheritance, psychic & occult matters, transformation, shared values, sexual energy, investigations

9th House: wisdom, justice, law, exploration, faith, religious & spiritual pursuits, higher education, foreign travel, legal action, experimentation, seeking truth

10th House: accomplishments, authority, recognition, success, reputation, professional affairs, maturity, mastery, honor, self-fulfillment, public life

11th House: groups & clubs, trends, friends, political awareness, emotional detachment, progressive thought, new technology & inventions, astrology

12th House: concern for others, self-sacrifice, psychological health, pre-natal imprinting, secret keeping, surrender, acceptance, spirituality

New Moon   **July 10**   **01:16**   **Moon 18°♋01'**   **Natal House_____**

                                              Sun   18°♋01'

What am I open to for the upcoming cycle? What is entering my awareness? What does my intuition bring? This is a contemplative outlook. Seedling/Germination

Moon & Sun in ♋ CANCER: nurturing, family oriented, watery, emotional, protective, psychic, domestic, sustaining, intuitive, sensitive, supportive, attached/connected

I emerge with _____

_____

_____

_____

_____

_____

_____

_____

My Tarot, Oracle, or Inspiration Card for New Moon Phase:_____

_____

_____

_____

_____

_____

_____

_____

_____

Crescent   **July 13**   **20:40**   **Moon 06°♍39'**   **Natal House_____**

                                                         Sun   21°♋39'   **Natal House_____**

What will I overcome that is worth letting go of? What are my resources? How do I prepare? What change am I resisting? This is preparedness outlook. Sprout

Moon in ♍ VIRGO: analytical, organized, efficient, health-conscious, conscientious, exacting, technical, healing, problem solving, scientific, time efficient

Sun in ♋ CANCER: nurturing, family oriented, watery, emotional, protective, psychic, domestic, sustaining, intuitive, sensitive, supportive, attached/connected

I challenge myself to _____

_____

_____

_____

_____

_____

_____

_____

My Tarot, Oracle, or Inspiration Card for Crescent Phase: _____

_____

_____

_____

_____

_____

_____

First Quarter   July 17   10:10   Moon 25°♎03'   Natal House_____
                                                           Sun   25°♋03'   Natal House_____

What steps will I take toward accomplishing my goals? How do I move forward in the next few days and/or long term? This is an action outlook. Root/Stem/Leaf – photosynthesis strengthens.
Moon in ♎ LIBRA: cooperative, fair, considerate, artistic, tasteful, diplomatic, tactful, impartial, refined, balanced, deliberate, soft-spoken, judgmental
Sun in ♋ CANCER: nurturing, family oriented, watery, emotional, protective, psychic, domestic, sustaining, intuitive, sensitive, supportive, attached/connected

I take action on _____

_____

_____

_____

_____

_____

_____

My Tarot, Oracle, or Inspirational Card for First Quarter Phase:_____

_____

_____

_____

_____

_____

_____

Gibbous July 20 19:05 Moon 13°♐16' Natal House_____

Sun 28°♋16' Natal House_____

How do I stay on track? What do I need to stay organized? What do I need to compromise if anything?
This is a maintenance outlook. Buds appear and develop in size.

Moon in ♐ SAGITTARIUS: expansive, philosophical, truth seeking, ethical, idealistic, optimistic, inspiring, wise, truth-seeking, motivational, truth speaking, honest

Sun in ♋ CANCER: nurturing, family oriented, watery, emotional, protective, psychic, domestic, sustaining, intuitive, sensitive, supportive, attached/connected

I develop structure with

_____

_____

_____

_____

_____

_____

_____

My Tarot, Oracle, or Inspirational Card for Gibbous Phase:_____

_____

_____

_____

_____

_____

_____

_____

◯ **Full**　　**July 24**　　**02:36**　　**Moon　01°♒26'**　　**Natal House**_____

　　　　　　　　　　　　　　　　　Sun　　01°♌26'　　**Natal House**_____

How do I see myself functioning in my world with my process? What does it look like within me and in my day to day world? This is a reflective outlook. Flower/Fruit

Moon in ♒ AQUARIUS: humanitarian, collective, innovative, progressive, eccentric, detached, electric, friendly, generous, gregarious, unpredictable, aloof

Sun in ♌ LEO: self-confident, dignified, generous, playful, dramatic, courageous, caring, radiant, romantic, loving, self-centered/focused, strong hearted, brave

I reflect fulfillment with

_____

_____

_____

_____

_____

_____

_____

My Tarot, Oracle, or Inspirational Card for Full Moon Phase: _____

_____

_____

_____

_____

_____

_____

_____

◑ **Disseminating** July 27   15:00   Moon 19° ♓ 47'   Natal House _____
                                              Sun   04° ♌ 47'   Natal House _____

How can I share my experiences? Where can I help others with my learning and experience?
This is a sharing outlook. First harvest.

Moon in ♓ PISCES: spiritual, subtle, empathic, visionary, sensitive, psychic, vulnerable, intuitive, self-sacrificing, indulgent, loving, artistic

Sun in ♌ LEO: self-confident, dignified, generous, playful, dramatic, courageous, caring, radiant, romantic, loving, self-centered/focused, strong hearted, brave

I share _____

_____

_____

_____

_____

_____

_____

My Tarot, Oracle, or Inspirational Card for Disseminating Phase: _____

_____

_____

_____

_____

_____

_____

Last Quarter   **July 31**   **13:15**   **Moon 08°♉33'**   **Natal House** _____

                                                                        Sun   08°♌33'   **Natal House** _____

How do I change or let go of the patterns that do not serve me and/or my community?
This is a reorienting outlook. Decay/Last Harvest and turning under of plant remains for composting.
Moon in ♉ TAURUS: sensual, physical, reliable, consistent, resourceful, deliberate, passive, practical, sensual, financial, valued, comfortable
Sun in ♌ LEO: self-confident, dignified, generous, playful, dramatic, courageous, caring, radiant, romantic, loving, self-centered/focused, strong hearted, brave

I change perspective on

_____

_____

_____

_____

_____

_____

_____

My Tarot, Oracle, or Inspirational Card for Last Quarter Phase:_____

_____

_____

_____

_____

_____

_____

_____

Balsamic   **August 4**   **16:18**   **Moon 27°♊30'**   **Natal House _____**
                                              Sun   12°♌30'   **Natal House _____**

How do I resolve the past Month and visualize, plan for up upcoming process? This is a pre-contemplative outlook. Seed is planted, released to develop next cycle/ germination begins.

Moon in ♊ GEMINI: Clever, versatile, agile, curious, articulate, alert, conversational, adaptable, lighthearted, happy, quick-witted, cheerful

Sun in ♌ LEO: self-confident, dignified, generous, playful, dramatic, courageous, caring, radiant, romantic, loving, self-centered/focused, strong hearted, brave

I resolve/release and/or plan

_____

_____

_____

_____

_____

_____

_____

My Tarot, Oracle, or Inspirational Card for the Balsamic Phase: _____

_____

_____

_____

_____

_____

_____

_____

♌ Leo 2021

EPHEMERIS at Midnight UTC	
8-Aug	08°Le46'
9-Aug	21°Le46'
10-Aug	05°Vi02'
11-Aug	18°Vi32'
12-Aug	02°Li13'
13-Aug	16°Li02'
14-Aug	29°Li59'
15-Aug	14°Sc01'
16-Aug	28°Sc07'
17-Aug	12°Sg16'
18-Aug	26°Sg28'
19-Aug	10°Cp40'
20-Aug	24°Cp49'
21-Aug	08°Aq52'
22-Aug	22°Aq44'
23-Aug	06°Pi22'
24-Aug	19°Pi42'
25-Aug	02°Ar42'
26-Aug	15°Ar22'
27-Aug	27°Ar44'
28-Aug	09°Ta50'
29-Aug	21°Ta46'
30-Aug	03°Ge35'
31-Aug	15°Ge24'
1-Sep	27°Ge17'
2-Sep	09°Cn20'
3-Sep	21°Cn38'
4-Sep	04°Le15'
5-Sep	17°Le12'
6-Sep	00°Vi30'
7-Sep	14°Vi08'

Chart House keywords are nouns.

1st House: my body, my identity, myself, my appearance, my projected image, my soul-purpose, my initial approach to life, my interests, my sense of me

2nd House: my talents, my resources, my values, my physical possessions, my money, my personal self-esteem, my sensuous enjoyment, myself worth

3rd House: my adaptability, my communications, my siblings, my neighborhood, short journey, my active search for knowledge, learning, curiosity, thinking

4th House: my home, family, heritage, my privacy, my emotional life, feelings, eating habits, receptivity, my protective urges, vulnerability

5th House: my abilities, my creative ability, pregnancy, children, pleasures, will power, romance, merry making, vacation, affection, confidence

6th House: my work conditions & habits, pets, my health, service offered, productivity, training, work skills, hygiene, clothing, nutrition & diet

7th House: agreements, contracts, partnerships, spouse, relationships, consultants, open enemies, receiving love, self-projection, social skills

8th House: loyalty, partner's money & resources, taxes, inheritance, psychic & occult matters, transformation, shared values, sexual energy, investigations

9th House: wisdom, justice, law, exploration, faith, religious & spiritual pursuits, higher education, foreign travel, legal action, experimentation, seeking truth

10th House: accomplishments, authority, recognition, success, reputation, professional affairs, maturity, mastery, honor, self-fulfillment, public life

11th House: groups & clubs, trends, friends, political awareness, emotional detachment, progressive thought, new technology & inventions, astrology

12th House: concern for others, self-sacrifice, psychological health, pre-natal imprinting, secret keeping, surrender, acceptance, spirituality

new   August 8   13:49   Moon 16° ♌ 14'   Natal House_____
                                        Sun   16° ♌ 14'

What am I open to for the upcoming cycle? What is entering my awareness? What does my intuition bring? This is a contemplative outlook. Seedling/Germination

Moon & Sun in ♌ LEO: self-confident, dignified, generous, playful, dramatic, courageous, caring, radiant, romantic, loving, self-centered/focused, strong hearted, brave

I emerge with

_____

_____

_____

_____

_____

_____

_____

My Tarot, Oracle, or Inspiration Card for New Moon Phase: _____

_____

_____

_____

_____

_____

_____

_____

◖ **Crescent**   **August 12**   **04:18**   **Moon 04°♎41'**   **Natal House**_____
                                                          Sun   19°♌41'   **Natal House**_____

What will I overcome that is worth letting go of? What are my resources? How do I prepare?
What change am I resisting? This is preparedness outlook. Sprout

Moon in ♎ LIBRA: cooperative, fair, considerate, artistic, tasteful, diplomatic, tactful, impartial, refined, balanced, deliberate, soft-spoken, judgmental

Sun ♌ LEO: self-confident, dignified, generous, playful, dramatic, courageous, caring, radiant, romantic, loving, generous, self-centered, strong hearted, brave

I challenge myself to
_____

_____

_____

_____

_____

_____

_____

_____

_____

My Tarot, Oracle, or Inspiration Card for Crescent Phase: _____

_____

_____

_____

_____

_____

_____

_____

_____

**First Quarter   August 15   15:19   Moon 23°♏ 00'   Natal House_____
                                                    Sun   23°♌ 00'   Natal House_____**

What steps will I take toward accomplishing my goals? How do I move forward in the next few days and/or long term? This is an action outlook. Root/Stem/Leaf – photosynthesis strengthens.
Moon in ♏ SCORPIO: transformational, magnetic, mysterious, hidden, sexual, erotic, secretive, musical, renewing, trust-worthy, loyal, supportive
Sun ♌ LEO: self-confident, dignified, generous, playful, dramatic, courageous, caring, radiant, romantic, loving, generous, self-centered, strong hearted, brave

I take action on

_____

_____

_____

_____

_____

_____

_____

My Tarot, Oracle, or Inspirational Card for First Quarter Phase: _____

_____

_____

_____

_____

_____

_____

_____

Gibbous   **August 19**   **01:02**   **Moon 11°♑17'**   **Natal House_____**
                                                      Sun 26°♌17'   **Natal House_____**

How do I stay on track? What do I need to stay organized? What do I need to compromise if anything? This is a maintenance outlook. Buds appear and develop in size.

Moon in ♑ CAPRICORN: authoritative, disciplined, realistic, responsible, practical, goal oriented, materialistic, successful, ambitious, professional, manifesting

Sun ♌ LEO: self-confident, dignified, generous, playful, dramatic, courageous, caring, radiant, romantic, loving, generous, self-centered, strong hearted, brave

I develop structure with _____

_____

_____

_____

_____

_____

_____

_____

My Tarot, Oracle, or Inspirational Card for Gibbous Phase: _____

_____

_____

_____

_____

_____

_____

_____

_____

◯ **Full   August 22   12:01   Moon 29°♒37'   Natal House_____**
                                              Sun   29°♌37'   Natal House_____

How do I see myself functioning in my world with my process? What does it look like within me and in my day to day world? This is a reflective outlook. Flower/Fruit

Moon in ♒AQUARIUS: humanitarian, collective, innovative, progressive, eccentric, detached, electric, friendly, generous, gregarious, unpredictable, aloof

Sun ♌ LEO: self-confident, dignified, generous, playful, dramatic, courageous, caring, radiant, romantic, loving, generous, self-centered, strong hearted, brave

I reflect fulfillment with _____

_____

_____

_____

_____

_____

_____

My Tarot, Oracle, or Inspirational Card for Full Moon Phase: _____

_____

_____

_____

_____

_____

_____

_____

◐ **Disseminating** **August 26** **05:26** **Moon 18°♈12'** **Natal House** _____

Sun 03°♍12' **Natal House** _____

How can I share my experiences? Where can I help others with my learning and experience?
this is a sharing outlook. First harvest.

Moon in ♈ ARIES: assertive, courageous, independent, passionate, athletic, enthusiastic, active, aggressive, initiating, focused, forward, direct

Sun ♍ VIRGO: analytical, organized, efficient, health-conscious, conscientious, exacting, technical, healing, problem solving, scientific, time efficient

I share _____

_____

_____

_____

_____

_____

_____

My Tarot, Oracle, or Inspirational Card for Disseminating Phase: _____

_____

_____

_____

_____

_____

_____

_____

◐ **Last Quarter** **August 30** **07:13**   **Moon** 07°♊08'   **Natal House** _____

                                                 Sun 07°♍08'   **Natal House** _____

How do I change or let go of the patterns that do not serve me and/or my community?
This is a reorienting outlook. Decay/Last Harvest and turning under of plant remains for composting.
Moon in ♊ GEMINI: Clever, versatile, agile, curious, articulate, alert, conversational, adaptable, lighthearted, happy, quick-witted, cheerful
Sun ♍ VIRGO: analytical, organized, efficient, health-conscious, conscientious, exacting, technical, healing, problem solving, scientific, time efficient

I change perspective on _____

_____

_____

_____

_____

_____

_____

My Tarot, Oracle, or Inspirational Card for Last Quarter Phase:_____

_____

_____

_____

_____

_____

_____

_____

Balsamic   **September 3**   **08:28**   **Moon 26°♋03'**   **Natal House** _____
                                                        Sun   11°♍03'   **Natal House** _____

How do I resolve the past Month and visualize, plan for up upcoming process? This is a pre-contemplative outlook. Seed is planted, released to develop next cycle/ germination begins.

Moon in ♋ CANCER: nurturing, family oriented, watery, emotional, protective, psychic, domestic, sustaining, intuitive, sensitive, supportive, attached/connected

Sun ♍ VIRGO: analytical, organized, efficient, health-conscious, conscientious, exacting, technical, healing, problem solving, scientific, time efficient

I resolve/release and/or plan

_____

_____

_____

_____

_____

_____

my Tarot, Oracle, or Inspirational Card for the Balsamic Phase: _____

_____

_____

_____

_____

_____

♍ Virgo 2021

EPHEMERIS at Midnight UTC		Chart House keywords are nouns.
7-Sep	14°Vi08'	**1st House:** my body, my identity, myself, my appearance, my projected image, my soul-purpose, my initial approach to life, my interests, my sense of me
8-Sep	28°Vi02'	
9-Sep	12°Li09'	**2nd House:** my talents, my resources, my values, my physical possessions, my money, my personal self-esteem, my sensuous enjoyment, myself worth
10-Sep	26°Li23'	
11-Sep	10°Sc39'	**3rd House:** my adaptability, my communications, my siblings, my neighborhood, short journey, my active search for knowledge, learning, curiosity, thinking
12-Sep	24°Sc55'	
13-Sep	09°Sg07'	
14-Sep	23°Sg13'	**4th House:** my home, family, heritage, my privacy, my emotional life, feelings, eating habits, receptivity, my protective urges, vulnerability
15-Sep	07°Cp14'	
16-Sep	21°Cp09'	
17-Sep	04°Aq55'	**5th House:** my abilities, my creative ability, pregnancy, children, pleasures, will power, romance, merry making, vacation, affection, confidence
18-Sep	18°Aq33'	
19-Sep	02°Pi01'	**6th House:** my work conditions & habits, pets, my health, service offered, productivity, training, work skills, hygiene, clothing, nutrition & diet
20-Sep	15°Pi16'	
21-Sep	28°Pi16'	
Equinox 22-Sep	11°Ar01'	**7th House:** agreements, contracts, partnerships, spouse, relationships, consultants, open enemies, receiving love, self-projection, social skills
23-Sep	23°Ar31'	
24-Sep	05°Ta46'	**8th House:** loyalty, partner's Money & resources, taxes, inheritance, psychic & occult matters, transformation, shared values, sexual energy, investigations
25-Sep	17°Ta48'	
26-Sep	29°Ta42'	
27-Sep	11°Ge30'	
28-Sep	23°Ge17'	**9th House:** wisdom, justice, law, exploration, faith, religious & spiritual pursuits, higher education, foreign travel, legal action, experimentation, seeking truth
29-Sep	05°Cn10'	
30-Sep	17°Cn13'	
1-Oct	29°Cn32'	**10th House:** accomplishments, authority, recognition, success, reputation, professional affairs, maturity, mastery, honor, self-fulfillment, public life
2-Oct	12°Le10'	
3-Oct	25°Le12'	**11th House:** groups & clubs, trends, friends, political awareness, emotional detachment, progressive thought, new technology & inventions, astrology
4-Oct	08°Vi39'	
5-Oct	22°Vi31'	**12th House:** concern for others, self-sacrifice, psychological health, pre-natal imprinting, secret keeping, surrender, acceptance, spirituality
6-Oct	06°Li44'	

New   **September 7**   **00:51**   **Moon 14°♍38'**   **Natal House_____**
                                           Sun   14°♍38'

What am I open to for the upcoming cycle? What is entering my awareness? What does my intuition bring? This is a contemplative outlook. Seedling/Germination

Moon & Sun ♍ VIRGO: analytical, organized, efficient, health-conscious, conscientious, exacting, technical, healing, problem solving, scientific, time efficient

I emerge with

_____

_____

_____

_____

_____

_____

_____

My Tarot, Oracle, or Inspiration Card for New Moon Phase: _____

_____

_____

_____

_____

_____

_____

_____

Crescent   September 10   11:03   Moon 02°♏ 57'   Natal House_____
                                                   Sun   17°♍57'   Natal House_____

What will I overcome that is worth letting go of? What are my resources? How do I prepare? What change am I resisting? This is preparedness outlook. Sprout

Moon in ♏ SCORPIO: transformational, magnetic, mysterious, hidden, sexual, erotic, secretive, musical, renewing, trust-worthy, loyal, supportive

Sun ♍ VIRGO: analytical, organized, efficient, health-conscious, conscientious, exacting, technical, healing, problem solving, scientific, time efficient

I challenge myself to

_____

_____

_____

_____

_____

_____

_____

_____

My Tarot, Oracle, or Inspiration Card for Crescent Phase: _____

_____

_____

_____

_____

_____

_____

First Quarter   September 13   **20:39**   **Moon 21°♐16'**   **Natal House_____**
                                                        Sun   21°♍16'   **Natal House_____**

What steps will I take toward accomplishing my goals? How do I move forward in the next few days and/or long term? This is an action outlook. Root/Stem/Leaf – photosynthesis strengthens.

Moon in ♐ SAGITTARIUS: expansive, philosophical, truth seeking, ethical, idealistic, optimistic, inspiring, wise, truth-seeking, motivational, truth speaking, honest

Sun in ♍ VIRGO: analytical, organized, efficient, health-conscious, conscientious, exacting, technical, healing, problem solving, scientific, time efficient

I take action on _____

_____

_____

_____

_____

_____

_____

My Tarot, Oracle, or Inspirational Card for First Quarter Phase: _____

_____

_____

_____

_____

_____

_____

_____

_____

Gibbous   **September 17**   08:18   **Moon 09°♒40'**   **Natal House_____**

                                                        Sun   24°♍40'   **Natal House_____**

How do I stay on track? What do I need to stay organized? What do I need to compromise if anything?
This is a maintenance outlook. Buds appear and develop in size.

Moon in ♒ AQUARIUS: humanitarian, collective, innovative, progressive, eccentric, detached,
electric, friendly, generous, gregarious, unpredictable, aloof

Sun in ♍ VIRGO: analytical, organized, efficient, health-conscious, conscientious, exacting, technical,
healing, problem solving, scientific, time efficient

I develop structure with
_____

_____

_____

_____

_____

_____

_____

_____

My Tarot, Oracle, or Inspirational Card for Gibbous Phase: _____

_____

_____

_____

_____

_____

_____

_____

◯ **Full**   **September 20**   **23:54**   **Moon 28°♓13'**   **Natal House**_____
                                                        Sun   28°♍13'   **Natal House**_____

How do I see myself functioning in my world with my process? What does it look like within me and in my day to day world? This is a reflective outlook. Flower/Fruit

Moon in ♓ PISCES: spiritual, subtle, empathic, visionary, sensitive, psychic, vulnerable, intuitive, self-sacrificing, indulgent, loving, artistic

Sun in ♍ VIRGO: analytical, organized, efficient, health-conscious, conscientious, exacting, technical, healing, problem solving, scientific, time efficient

I reflect fulfillment with _____

_____

_____

_____

_____

_____

_____

my Tarot, Oracle, or Inspirational Card for Full Moon Phase: _____

_____

_____

_____

_____

_____

_____

Disseminating   September 24   22:32   **Moon 17°♉05'**   **Natal House** _____

                                                          Sun   02°♎05'   **Natal House** _____

how can I share my experiences? Where can I help others with my learning and experience?
this is a sharing outlook. First harvest.

Moon in ♉ TAURUS: sensual, physical, reliable, consistent, resourceful, deliberate, passive, practical, sensual, financial, valued, comfortable

Sun in ♎ LIBRA: analytical, organized, efficient, health-conscious, conscientious, exacting, technical, healing, problem solving, scientific, time efficient

I share _____

_____

_____

_____

_____

_____

_____

My Tarot, Oracle, or Inspirational Card for Disseminating Phase: _____

_____

_____

_____

_____

_____

_____

Last Quarter   **September 29**   01:56   **Moon 06°♋08'**   **Natal House** _____

                                                  Sun 06°♎08'   **Natal House** _____

How do I change or let go of the patterns that do not serve me and/or my community?
This is a reorienting outlook. Decay/Last Harvest and turning under of plant remains for composting.
Moon in ♋ CANCER: nurturing, family oriented, watery, emotional, protective, psychic, domestic, sustaining, intuitive, sensitive, supportive, attached/connected
Sun in ♎ LIBRA: cooperative, fair, considerate, artistic, tasteful, diplomatic, tactful, impartial, refined, balanced, deliberate, soft-spoken, judgmental

I change perspective on

My Tarot, Oracle, or Inspirational Card for Last Quarter Phase:_____

Balsamic **October 2** **23:35** **Moon 24°♌59'** **Natal House** _____

Sun 09°♎59' **Natal House** _____

How do I resolve the past Month and visualize, plan for up upcoming process? This is a pre-contemplative outlook. Seed is planted, released to develop next cycle/ germination begins.

Moon in ♌ LEO: self-confident, dignified, generous, playful, dramatic, courageous, caring, radiant, romantic, loving, self-centered/focused, strong hearted, brave

Sun in ♎ LIBRA: cooperative, fair, considerate, artistic, tasteful, diplomatic, tactful, impartial, refined, balanced, deliberate, soft-spoken, judgmental

I resolve/release and/or plan _____

_____

_____

_____

_____

_____

_____

My Tarot, Oracle, or Inspirational Card for the Balsamic Phase: _____

_____

_____

_____

_____

_____

♎ Libra 2021

EPHEMERIS at MIDNIGHT UTC		Chart House keywords are nouns.
6-Oct	06°Li44'	**1st House:** my body, my identity, myself, my appearance, my projected image, my soul-purpose, my initial approach to life, my interests, my sense of me
7-Oct	21°Li14'	
8-Oct	05°Sc53'	
9-Oct	20°Sc35'	**2nd House:** my talents, my resources, my values, my physical possessions, my money, my personal self-esteem, my sensuous enjoyment, myself worth
10-Oct	05°Sg13'	
11-Oct	19°Sg42'	
12-Oct	03°Cp59'	**3rd House:** my adaptability, my communications, my siblings, my neighborhood, short journey, my active search for knowledge, learning, curiosity, thinking
13-Oct	18°Cp02'	
14-Oct	01°Aq49'	
15-Oct	15°Aq23'	**4th House:** my home, family, heritage, my privacy, my emotional life, feelings, eating habits, receptivity, my protective urges, vulnerability
16-Oct	28°Aq42'	
17-Oct	11°Pi47'	**5th House:** my abilities, my creative ability, pregnancy, children, pleasures, will power, romance, merry making, vacation, affection, confidence
18-Oct	24°Pi39'	
19-Oct	07°Ar19'	
20-Oct	19°Ar46'	**6th House:** my work conditions & habits, pets, my health, service offered, productivity, training, work skills, hygiene, clothing, nutrition & diet
21-Oct	02°Ta02'	
22-Oct	14°Ta07'	
23-Oct	26°Ta04'	**7th House:** agreements, contracts, partnerships, spouse, relationships, consultants, open enemies, receiving love, self-projection, social skills
24-Oct	07°Ge54'	
25-Oct	19°Ge41'	**8th House:** loyalty, partner's money & resources, taxes, inheritance, psychic & occult matters, transformation, shared values, sexual energy, investigations
26-Oct	01°Cn28'	
27-Oct	13°Cn20'	
28-Oct	25°Cn22'	**9th House:** wisdom, justice, law, exploration, faith, religious & spiritual pursuits, higher education, foreign travel, legal action, experimentation, seeking truth
29-Oct	07°Le38'	
30-Oct	20°Le13'	**10th House:** accomplishments, authority, recognition, success, reputation, professional affairs, maturity, mastery, honor, self-fulfillment, public life
31-Oct	03°Vi11'	
1-Nov	16°Vi36'	
2-Nov	00°Li28'	**11th House:** groups & clubs, trends, friends, political awareness, emotional detachment, progressive thought, new technology & inventions, astrology
3-Nov	14°Li47'	
4-Nov	29°Li27'	
		12th House: concern for others, self-sacrifice, psychological health, pre-natal imprinting, secret keeping, surrender, acceptance, spirituality

New   October 6   11:05   Moon 13°♎24'   Natal House_____
                                            Sun   13°♎24'

What am I open to for the upcoming cycle? What is entering my awareness? What does my intuition bring? This is a contemplative outlook. Seedling/Germination

Moon & Sun in ♎ LIBRA: cooperative, fair, considerate, artistic, tasteful, diplomatic, tactful, impartial, refined, balanced, deliberate, soft-spoken, judgmental

I emerge with _____

_____

_____

_____

_____

_____

_____

My Tarot, Oracle, or Inspiration Card for New Moon Phase: _____

_____

_____

_____

_____

_____

Crescent   **October 9**   **18:08**   **Moon 01°♐39'**   **Natal House_____**
                                                      Sun   16°♎39'   **Natal House_____**

What will I overcome that is worth letting go of? What are my resources? How do I prepare? What change am I resisting? This is preparedness outlook. Sprout

Moon in ♐ SAGITTARIUS: expansive, philosophical, truth seeking, ethical, idealistic, optimistic, inspiring, wise, truth-seeking, motivational, truth speaking, honest

Sun in ♎ LIBRA: cooperative, fair, considerate, artistic, tasteful, diplomatic, tactful, impartial, refined, balanced, deliberate, soft-spoken, judgmental

I challenge myself to _____

_____

_____

_____

_____

_____

_____

_____

My Tarot, Oracle, or Inspiration Card for Crescent Phase: _____

_____

_____

_____

_____

_____

_____

First Quarter   October 13   03:24   Moon 20°♑00'   Natal House_____
                                               Sun   20°♎00'   Natal House_____

What steps will I take toward accomplishing my goals? How do I move forward in the next few days and/or long term? This is an action outlook. Root/Stem/Leaf – photosynthesis strengthens.

Moon in ♑ CAPRICORN: authoritative, disciplined, realistic, responsible, practical, goal oriented, materialistic, successful, ambitious, professional, manifesting

Sun in ♎ LIBRA: cooperative, fair, considerate, artistic, tasteful, diplomatic, tactful, impartial, refined, balanced, deliberate, soft-spoken, judgmental

I take action on _____

_____

_____

_____

_____

_____

_____

My Tarot, Oracle, or Inspirational Card for First Quarter Phase:_____

_____

_____

_____

_____

_____

_____

Gibbous   October 16   18:05   Moon 08°♓35'   Natal House_____

Sun   23°♎35'   Natal House_____

How do I stay on track? What do I need to stay organized? What do I need to compromise if anything? This is a maintenance outlook. Buds appear and develop in size.

Moon in ♓ PISCES: spiritual, subtle, empathic, visionary, sensitive, psychic, vulnerable, intuitive, self-sacrificing, indulgent, loving, artistic

Sun in ♎ LIBRA: cooperative, fair, considerate, artistic, tasteful, diplomatic, tactful, impartial, refined, balanced, deliberate, soft-spoken, judgmental

I develop structure with

_____

_____

_____

_____

_____

_____

_____

My Tarot, Oracle, or Inspirational Card for Gibbous Phase: _____

_____

_____

_____

_____

_____

_____

_____

◯ **Full**   **October 20**   **14:56**   **Moon 27°♈26'**   **Natal House_____**

                                                        Sun   27°♎26'   **Natal House_____**

How do I see myself functioning in my world with my process? What does it look like within me and in my day to day world? This is a reflective outlook. Flower/Fruit

Moon in♈ ARIES: assertive, courageous, independent, passionate, athletic, enthusiastic, active, aggressive, initiating, focused, forward, direct

Sun in ♎ LIBRA: cooperative, fair, considerate, artistic, tasteful, diplomatic, tactful, impartial, refined, balanced, deliberate, soft-spoken, judgmental

I reflect fulfillment with _____

_____

_____

_____

_____

_____

_____

My Tarot, Oracle, or Inspirational Card for Full Moon Phase: _____

_____

_____

_____

_____

_____

◑ **Disseminating   October 24   17:32   Moon 16°♊31'   Natal House _____**
                                                    Sun   01°♏31'   Natal House _____

How can I share my experiences? Where can I help others with my learning and experience?
This is a sharing outlook. First harvest.

Moon in ♊ GEMINI: Clever, versatile, agile, curious, articulate, alert, conversational, adaptable, lighthearted, happy, quick-witted, cheerful

Sun in ♏ SCORPIO: transformational, magnetic, mysterious, hidden, sexual, erotic, secretive, musical, renewing, trust-worthy, loyal, supportive

I share _____

_____

_____

_____

_____

_____

_____

My Tarot, Oracle, or Inspirational Card for Disseminating Phase: _____

_____

_____

_____

_____

_____

_____

_____

◑ **Last Quarter** **October 28** **20:05** **Moon** 05°♌37' **Natal House** _____
Sun 05°♏37' **Natal House** _____

How do I change or let go of the patterns that do not serve me and/or my community?
This is a reorienting outlook. Decay/Last Harvest and turning under of plant remains for composting.
Moon in ♌ LEO: self-confident, dignified, generous, playful, dramatic, courageous, caring, radiant, romantic, loving, self-centered/focused, strong hearted, brave
Sun in ♏ SCORPIO: transformational, magnetic, mysterious, hidden, sexual, erotic, secretive, musical, renewing, trust-worthy, loyal, supportive

I change perspective on _____

_____

_____

_____

_____

_____

_____

My Tarot, Oracle, or Inspirational Card for Last Quarter Phase:_____

_____

_____

_____

_____

_____

_____

Balsamic   November 1   13:28   Moon 24°♍20'   Natal House _____

                                          Sun   09°♏20'   Natal House _____

How do I resolve the past Month and visualize, plan for up upcoming process? This is a pre-contemplative outlook. Seed is planted, released to develop next cycle/ germination begins.

Moon in ♍ VIRGO: analytical, organized, efficient, health-conscious, conscientious, exacting, technical, healing, problem solving, scientific, time efficient

Sun in ♏ SCORPIO: transformational, magnetic, mysterious, hidden, sexual, erotic, secretive, musical, renewing, trust-worthy, loyal, supportive

I resolve/release and/or plan _____

_____

_____

_____

_____

_____

_____

My Tarot, Oracle, or Inspirational Card for the Balsamic Phase: _____

_____

_____

_____

_____

_____

_____

♏ Scorpio 2021 Partial Lunar Eclipse

EPHEMERIS at MIDNIGHT UTC		Chart House keywords are nouns.
4-Nov	29°Li27'	**1st House:** my body, my identity, myself, my appearance, my projected image, my soul-purpose, my initial approach to life, my interests, my sense of me
5-Nov	14°Sc23'	
6-Nov	29°Sc27'	
7-Nov	14°Sg28'	**2nd House:** my talents, my resources, my values, my physical possessions, my money, my personal self-esteem, my sensuous enjoyment, my self-worth
8-Nov	29°Sg21'	
9-Nov	13°Cp57'	
10-Nov	28°Cp12'	**3rd House:** my adaptability, my communications, my siblings, my neighborhood, short journey, my active search for knowledge, learning, curiosity, thinking
11-Nov	12°Aq06'	
12-Nov	25°Aq37'	
13-Nov	08°Pi48'	**4th House:** my home, family, heritage, my privacy, my emotional life, feelings, eating habits, receptivity, my protective urges, vulnerability
14-Nov	21°Pi40'	
15-Nov	04°Ar16'	**5th House:** my abilities, my creative ability, pregnancy, children, pleasures, will power, romance, merry making, vacation, affection, confidence
16-Nov	16°Ar39'	
17-Nov	28°Ar50'	
18-Nov	10°Ta53'	**6th House:** my work conditions & habits, pets, my health, service offered, productivity, training, work skills, hygiene, clothing, nutrition & diet
19-Nov	22°Ta48'	
20-Nov	04°Ge39'	**7th House:** agreements, contracts, partnerships, spouse, relationships, consultants, open enemies, receiving love, self-projection, social skills
21-Nov	16°Ge27'	
22-Nov	28°Ge15'	
23-Nov	10°Cn04'	**8th House:** loyalty, partner's money & resources, taxes, inheritance, psychic & occult matters, transformation, shared values, sexual energy, investigations
24-Nov	21°Cn59'	
25-Nov	04°Le03'	**9th House:** wisdom, justice, law, exploration, faith, religious & spiritual pursuits, higher education, foreign travel, legal action, experimentation, seeking truth
26-Nov	16°Le18'	
27-Nov	28°Le50'	
28-Nov	11°Vi42'	**10th House:** accomplishments, authority, recognition, success, reputation, professional affairs, maturity, mastery, honor, self-fulfillment, public life
29-Nov	24°Vi57'	
30-Nov	08°Li39'	
1-Dec	22°Li48'	**11th House:** groups & clubs, trends, friends, political awareness, emotional detachment, progressive thought, new technology & inventions, astrology
2-Dec	07°Sc22'	
3-Dec	22°Sc18'	**12th House:** concern for others, self-sacrifice, psychological health, pre-natal imprinting, secret keeping, surrender, acceptance, spirituality
4-Dec	07°Sg28'	

New   **November 4**   **21:14**   **Moon 12°♏ 40'**   **Natal House_____**
                                                            Sun   12°♏ 40'

What am I open to for the upcoming cycle? What is entering my awareness? What does my intuition bring? This is a contemplative outlook. Seedling/Germination

Moon & Sun in ♏ SCORPIO: transformational, magnetic, mysterious, hidden, sexual, erotic, secretive, musical, renewing, trust-worthy, loyal, supportive

I emerge with _____

_____

_____

_____

_____

_____

_____

My Tarot, Oracle, or Inspiration Card for New Moon Phase: _____

_____

_____

_____

_____

_____

_____

_____

_____

Crescent   November 8   02:31   Moon 00°♑54'   Natal House_____

Sun   15°♏54'   Natal House_____

What will I overcome that is worth letting go of? What are my resources? How do I prepare? What change am I resisting? This is preparedness outlook. Sprout

Moon in ♑ CAPRICORN: authoritative, disciplined, realistic, responsible, practical, goal oriented, materialistic, successful, ambitious, professional, manifesting

Sun in ♏ SCORPIO: transformational, magnetic, mysterious, hidden, sexual, erotic, secretive, musical, renewing, trust-worthy, loyal, supportive

I challenge myself to
_____

_____

_____

_____

_____

_____

_____

_____

My Tarot, Oracle, or Inspiration Card for Crescent Phase: _____

_____

_____

_____

_____

_____

_____

First Quarter   **November 11**   **12:45**   **Moon 19°♒20'**   **Natal House_____**

                                                                  Sun   19°♏20'   **Natal House_____**

What steps will I take toward accomplishing my goals? How do I move forward in the next few days and/or long term? This is an action outlook. Root/Stem/Leaf – photosynthesis strengthens.

Moon in ♒ AQUARIUS: humanitarian, collective, innovative, progressive, eccentric, detached, electric, friendly, generous, gregarious, unpredictable, aloof

Sun in ♏ SCORPIO: transformational, magnetic, mysterious, hidden, sexual, erotic, secretive, musical, renewing, trust-worthy, loyal, supportive

I take action on

_____

_____

_____

_____

_____

_____

_____

_____

My Tarot, Oracle, or Inspirational Card for First Quarter Phase: _____

_____

_____

_____

_____

_____

_____

◐ **Gibbous**   **November 15**   **07:27**   Moon **08°♈08'**   **Natal House**_____

                                                 Sun   **23°♏08'**   **Natal House**_____

How do I stay on track? What do I need to stay organized? What do I need to compromise if anything? This is a maintenance outlook. Buds appear and develop in size.

Moon in ♈ ARIES: assertive, courageous, independent, passionate, athletic, enthusiastic, active, aggressive, initiating, focused, forward, direct

Sun in ♏ SCORPIO: transformational, magnetic, mysterious, hidden, sexual, erotic, secretive, musical, renewing, trust-worthy, loyal, supportive

I develop structure with

_____

_____

_____

_____

_____

_____

_____

My Tarot, Oracle, or Inspirational Card for Gibbous Phase: _____

_____

_____

_____

_____

_____

_____

_____

Partial Lunar Eclipse

Full   November 19   08:57   Moon 27° ♉ 14'   Natal House_____

                                                Sun   27° ♏ 14'   Natal House_____

How do I see myself functioning in my world with my process? What does it look like within me and in my day to day world? This is a reflective outlook. Flower/Fruit

Moon in ♉ TAURUS: sensual, physical, reliable, consistent, resourceful, deliberate, passive, practical, sensual, financial, valued, comfortable

Sun in ♏ SCORPIO: transformational, magnetic, mysterious, hidden, sexual, erotic, secretive, musical, renewing, trust-worthy, loyal, supportive

I reflect fulfillment with

_____

_____

_____

_____

_____

_____

_____

_____

My Tarot, Oracle, or Inspirational Card for Full Moon Phase:_____

_____

_____

_____

_____

_____

_____

◗ Disseminating   **November 23**   **12:50**   Moon **16°♋26'**   Natal House _____
                                                    Sun   **01°♐26'**   Natal House _____

How can I share my experiences? Where can I help others with my learning and experience?
this is a sharing outlook. First harvest.

Moon in ♋ CANCER: nurturing, family oriented, watery, emotional, protective, psychic, domestic, sustaining, intuitive, sensitive, supportive, attached/connected

Sun in ♐ SAGITTARIUS: expansive, philosophical, truth seeking, ethical, idealistic, optimistic, inspiring, wise, truth-seeking, motivational, truth speaking, honest

I share
_____

_____

_____

_____

_____

_____

_____

My Tarot, Oracle, or Inspirational Card for Disseminating Phase: _____

_____

_____

_____

_____

_____

_____

_____

_____

Last Quarter   November 27   12:27   Moon 05°♍28'   Natal House _____
                                                      Sun   05°♐28'   Natal House _____

How do I change or let go of the patterns that do not serve me and/or my community?
this is a reorienting outlook. Decay/Last Harvest and turning under of plant remains for composting.
Moon in ♍ VIRGO: analytical, organized, efficient, health-conscious, conscientious, exacting, technical, healing, problem solving, scientific, time efficient
Sun in ♐ SAGITTARIUS: expansive, philosophical, truth seeking, ethical, idealistic, optimistic, inspiring, wise, truth-seeking, motivational, truth speaking, honest

I change perspective on

_____

_____

_____

_____

_____

_____

_____

My Tarot, Oracle, or Inspirational Card for Last Quarter Phase:_____

_____

_____

_____

_____

_____

_____

_____

_____

Balsamic   December 1   02:07   Moon 24°♎05'   Natal House _____
                                                        Sun   09°♐05'   Natal House _____

How do I resolve the past Month and visualize, plan for up upcoming process? This is a pre-contemplative outlook. Seed is planted, released to develop next cycle/ germination begins.

Moon in ♎ LIBRA: cooperative, fair, considerate, artistic, tasteful, diplomatic, tactful, impartial, refined, balanced, deliberate, soft-spoken, judgmental

Sun in ♐ SAGITTARIUS: expansive, philosophical, truth seeking, ethical, idealistic, optimistic, inspiring, wise, truth-seeking, motivational, truth speaking, honest

I resolve/release and/or plan _____

_____

_____

_____

_____

_____

_____

My Tarot, Oracle, or Inspirational Card for the Balsamic Phase: _____

_____

_____

_____

_____

_____

_____

_____

♐ Sagittarius 2021 Total Solar Eclipse

EPHEMERIS at MIDNIGHT UTC		Chart House keywords are nouns.
4-Dec	07°Sg28'	
5-Dec	22°Sg42'	**1st House:** my body, my identity, myself, my appearance, my projected image, my soul-purpose, my initial approach to life, my interests, my sense of me
6-Dec	07°Cp52'	
7-Dec	22°Cp47'	**2nd House:** my talents, my resources, my values, my physical possessions, my money, my personal self-esteem, my sensuous enjoyment, my self-worth
8-Dec	07°Aq20'	
9-Dec	21°Aq28'	
10-Dec	05°Pi08'	**3rd House:** my adaptability, my communications, my siblings, my neighborhood, short journey, my active search for knowledge, learning, curiosity, thinking
11-Dec	18°Pi21'	
12-Dec	01°Ar10'	
13-Dec	13°Ar39'	**4th House:** my home, family, heritage, my privacy, my emotional life, feelings, eating habits, receptivity, my protective urges, vulnerability
14-Dec	25°Ar53'	
15-Dec	07°Ta54'	**5th House:** my abilities, my creative ability, pregnancy, children, pleasures, will power, romance, merry making, vacation, affection, confidence
16-Dec	19°Ta47'	
17-Dec	01°Ge37'	
18-Dec	13°Ge24'	**6th House:** my work conditions & habits, pets, my health, service offered, productivity, training, work skills, hygiene, clothing, nutrition & diet
19-Dec	25°Ge13'	
20-Dec	07°Cn04'	**7th House:** agreements, contracts, partnerships, spouse, relationships, consultants, open enemies, receiving love, self-projection, social skills
Solstice 21-Dec	19°Cn00'	
22-Dec	01°Le03'	
23-Dec	13°Le15'	**8th House:** loyalty, partner's money & resources, taxes, inheritance, psychic & occult matters, transformation, shared values, sexual energy, investigations
24-Dec	25°Le37'	
25-Dec	08°Vi12'	**9th House:** wisdom, justice, law, exploration, faith, religious & spiritual pursuits, higher education, foreign travel, legal action, experimentation, seeking truth
26-Dec	21°Vi02'	
27-Dec	04°Li12'	
28-Dec	17°Li42'	**10th House:** accomplishments, authority, recognition, success, reputation, professional affairs, maturity, mastery, honor, self-fulfillment, public life
29-Dec	01°Sc35'	
30-Dec	15°Sc52'	
31-Dec	00°Sg31'	**11th House:** groups & clubs, trends, friends, political awareness, emotional detachment, progressive thought, new technology & inventions, astrology
Jan 1 2022	15°Sg28	
Jan 2 2022	00°Cp36	
		12th House: concern for others, self-sacrifice, psychological health, pre-natal imprinting, secret keeping, surrender, acceptance, spirituality

Total Solar Eclipse

New	December 4	07:42	Moon	12°♐22'	Natal House_____
			Sun	12°♐22'	

What am I open to for the upcoming cycle? What is entering my awareness? What does my intuition bring? This is a contemplative outlook. Seedling/Germination

Moon & Sun in ♐ SAGITTARIUS: expansive, philosophical, truth seeking, ethical, idealistic, optimistic, inspiring, wise, truth-seeking, motivational, truth speaking, honest

I emerge with

_____

_____

_____

_____

_____

_____

_____

_____

My Tarot, Oracle, or Inspiration Card for New Moon Phase: _____

_____

_____

_____

_____

_____

_____

_____

_____

Crescent   December 7   12:50   Moon 00°♒37'   Natal House_____
                                              Sun   15°♐37'   Natal House_____

What will I overcome that is worth letting go of? What are my resources? How do I prepare? What change am I resisting? This is preparedness outlook. Sprout

Moon in ♒ AQUARIUS: humanitarian, collective, innovative, progressive, eccentric, detached, electric, friendly, generous, gregarious, unpredictable, aloof

Sun in ♐ SAGITTARIUS: expansive, philosophical, truth seeking, ethical, idealistic, optimistic, inspiring, wise, truth-seeking, motivational, truth speaking, honest

I challenge myself to
_____
_____
_____
_____
_____
_____
_____
_____
_____

My Tarot, Oracle, or Inspiration Card for Crescent Phase: _____
_____
_____
_____
_____
_____
_____

First Quarter   **December 11**   **01:35**   **Moon 19°♓13'**   Natal House_____

                                                                Sun   **19°♐13'**   Natal House_____

What steps will I take toward accomplishing my goals? How do I move forward in the next few days and/or long term? This is an action outlook. Root/Stem/Leaf – photosynthesis strengthens.

Moon in ♓ PISCES: spiritual, subtle, empathic, visionary, sensitive, psychic, vulnerable, intuitive, self-sacrificing, indulgent, loving, artistic

Sun in ♐ SAGITTARIUS: expansive, philosophical, truth seeking, ethical, idealistic, optimistic, inspiring, wise, truth-seeking, motivational, truth speaking, honest

I take action on _____

_____

_____

_____

_____

_____

_____

My Tarot, Oracle, or Inspirational Card for First Quarter Phase: _____

_____

_____

_____

_____

_____

_____

_____

_____

Gibbous   **December 15**   **00:40**   **Moon 08° ♉ 14'**   **Natal House**_____

                                                              Sun   23° ♐ 14'   **Natal House**_____

How do I stay on track? What do I need to stay organized? What do I need to compromise if anything? This is a maintenance outlook. Buds appear and develop in size.

Moon in ♉ TAURUS: sensual, physical, reliable, consistent, resourceful, deliberate, passive, practical, sensual, financial, valued, comfortable

Sun in ♐ SAGITTARIUS: expansive, philosophical, truth seeking, ethical, idealistic, optimistic, inspiring, wise, truth-seeking, motivational, truth speaking, honest

I develop structure with

_____

_____

_____

_____

_____

_____

_____

My Tarot, Oracle, or Inspirational Card for Gibbous Phase:_____

_____

_____

_____

_____

_____

_____

Full   **December 19**   **04:35**   **Moon 27° Ⅱ 28'**   **Natal House**_____

                                                          Sun   27° ♐ 28'   **Natal House**_____

How do I see myself functioning in my world with my process? What does it look like within me and in my day to day world? This is a reflective outlook. Flower/Fruit

Moon in Ⅱ GEMINI: Clever, versatile, agile, curious, articulate, alert, conversational, adaptable, lighthearted, happy, quick-witted, cheerful

Sun in ♐ SAGITTARIUS: expansive, philosophical, truth seeking, ethical, idealistic, optimistic, inspiring, wise, truth-seeking, motivational, truth speaking, honest

I reflect fulfillment with _____

_____

_____

_____

_____

_____

_____

My Tarot, Oracle, or Inspirational Card for Full Moon Phase: _____

_____

_____

_____

_____

_____

_____

Disseminating   December 23   06:36   Moon 16°♌38'   Natal House _____
                                                   Sun   01°♑38'   Natal House _____

How can I share my experiences? Where can I help others with my learning and experience?
This is a sharing outlook. First harvest.

Moon in ♌ LEO: self-confident, dignified, generous, playful, dramatic, courageous, caring, radiant, romantic, loving, self-centered/focused, strong hearted, brave

Sun in ♑ CAPRICORN: authoritative, disciplined, realistic, responsible, practical, goal oriented, materialistic, successful, ambitious, professional, manifesting

I share _____

_____

_____

_____

_____

_____

_____

My Tarot, Oracle, or Inspirational Card for Disseminating Phase: _____

_____

_____

_____

_____

_____

_____

Last Quarter   **December 27**   **02:23**   **Moon 05°♎32'**   **Natal House** _____

Sun   05°♑32'   **Natal House** _____

How do I change or let go of the patterns that do not serve me and/or my community?
This is a reorienting outlook. Decay/Last Harvest and turning under of plant remains for composting.
Moon in ♎ LIBRA: cooperative, fair, considerate, artistic, tasteful, diplomatic, tactful, impartial, refined, balanced, deliberate, soft-spoken, judgmental
Sun in ♑ CAPRICORN: authoritative, disciplined, realistic, responsible, practical, goal oriented, materialistic, successful, ambitious, professional, manifesting

I change perspective on
_____

_____

_____

_____

_____

_____

_____

My Tarot, Oracle, or Inspirational Card for Last Quarter Phase:_____

_____

_____

_____

_____

_____

_____

_____

Balsamic   December 30   13:27   Moon 24°♏03'   Natal House _____
                                              Sun   09°♑03'   Natal House _____

How do I resolve the past Month and visualize, plan for up upcoming process? This is a pre-contemplative outlook. Seed is planted, released to develop next cycle/ germination begins.

Moon in ♏ SCORPIO: transformational, magnetic, mysterious, hidden, sexual, erotic, secretive, musical, renewing, trust-worthy, loyal, supportive

Sun in ♑ CAPRICORN: authoritative, disciplined, realistic, responsible, practical, goal oriented, materialistic, successful, ambitious, professional, manifesting

I resolve/release and/or plan

_____

_____

_____

_____

_____

_____

_____

My Tarot, Oracle, or Inspirational Card for the Balsamic Phase: _____

_____

_____

_____

_____

_____

_____

_____

Time Zone Conversion

- The Green Mountain Moon Journal Basic Version is created in Coordinated Universal Time (UTC or UT), using the Tropical Zodiac.

- Please note that no matter which time zone you live in, the zodiac degrees of the moon's phase are the same.

- When you know the plus+ or minus - from UTC of your own time zone is, each phase time can be easily adjusted; further adjustment may be needed if Daylight Savings or other seasonal time changes are used in your particular time zone. UTC does not use Daylight Savings Time but stays constant. It is the same as GMT (Greenwich Mean Time).

Here are some online links for Time Zone Conversion and Moon Phase Calculation:

TIME ZONE LIST: https://www.timeanddate.com/time/zones/

INTERACTIVE CALCULATOR: https://www.timeanddate.com/time/map/

Through the phases,
Mary Anna Abuzahra,
greenmountainintuitivearts.com

www.ingramcontent.com/pod-product-compliance
Lightning Source LLC
LaVergne TN
LVHW061301060426
835509LV00016B/1662